THE AMERICAN CENTURY SERIES

PEMBROKE

IN THE TWENTIETH CENTURY

THE AMERICAN CENTURY SERIES

PEMBROKE
IN THE TWENTIETH CENTURY

Connee Brayboy

ARCADIA PUBLISHING

ISBN 978-0-7385-9037-1

Published by Arcadia Publishing
Charleston, South Carolina

Printed in the United States of America

Library of Congress Catalog Card Number: 98-89164

For all general information contact Arcadia Publishing at:
Telephone 843-853-2070
Fax 843-853-0044
E-mail sales@arcadiapublishing.com
For customer service and orders:
Toll-Free 1-888-313-2665

Visit us on the Internet at www.arcadiapublishing.com

Contents

Introduction 6

1. Local Faces 11

2. Places of Worship and Religious Leaders 33

3. Businesses and Local Government 55

4. Schools and Education 77

5. Recreation 87

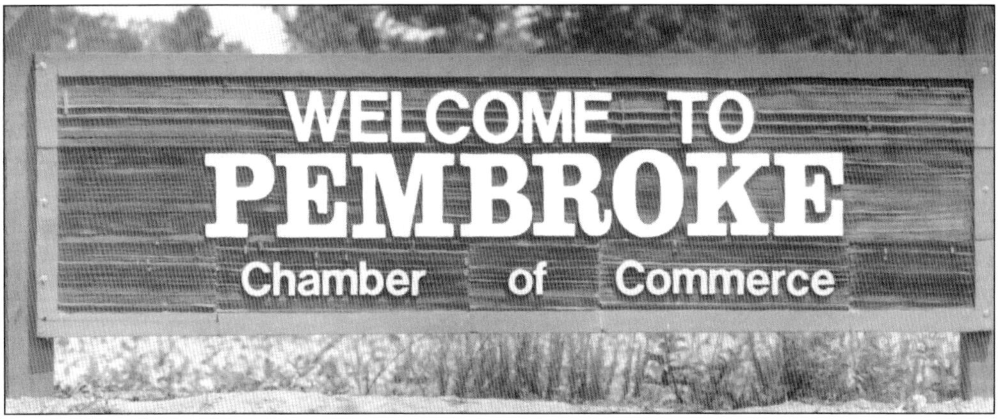

The "Welcome to Pembroke" signs were some of the public relations additions carried out by the Pembroke Chamber of Commerce. The signs are elevated to provide better visibility.

INTRODUCTION

Pembroke and the Lumbee Indians

The Lumbee, the largest tribe of Native Americans in North Carolina, is also the largest tribe east of the Mississippi. There are several communities that are historically recognized as Lumbee, and most of these communities are within a 7-mile radius of the town limits of Pembroke, North Carolina. These communities are old and have been considered home by the Lumbee for hundreds of years. In the traditional way, the extended families of the natives have lived for generations on the same land. In many instances, the parents and grandparents were born and reared on what is referred to by the Lumbee as "the Home Place," a Lumbee term meaning that the same family has owned the property for decades.

Lying in the western portion of Robeson County, Pembroke, is what has historically been called "Scuffletown." The boundaries of "Scuffletown" cannot be defined because it was not the custom of native people to define geographic boundaries. While the boundaries were not identifiable by non-Indians, the Lumbee Tribe has no difficulty understanding the boundaries of their home community.

Eventually, outlying Lumbee communities moved closer and closer to what is now incorporated as Pembroke. The 1850 census identifies three major distinct Native American communities in Robeson: Saddletree, Fairgrove, and Prospect. While the Saddletree and Fairgrove communities are more than 10 miles from the Pembroke area, they are very viable and distinct Native American communities. Several other communities within the 7-mile radius of Pembroke are also Lumbee communities. They are, more specifically, Prospect, Union Chapel, Deep Branch, and Mt. Airy, and they all have schools and churches that are almost totally Native American. Union Elementary is only one of several communities that has grown up around a school and does not have a church named for the community. Though the communities of Evans Crossings, Brooks' Settlement, Red Banks, Moss Neck, and Pates do not have a school or a church named after them, they are recognized as very distinct and traditional portions of the larger "Scuffletown." This designation is more an identification of families and clans, while the incorporated limits of Pembroke are recognized as the geographic, economic, and educational center of Native American country.

According to the 1990 census, there are more than 40,000 Native Americans residing in Robeson County who identify themselves as Lumbee. They consider Robeson County home and can trace their ancestors by name back before the first Europeans landed in the area. In spite of assimilation, education, and very advanced strategic thinking and political success, the Lumbee remain a very separate and distinct culture, maintaining pride in their home churches and schools. They are a proud people who separated by choice, recognizing soon after the first European contact that separating themselves and continuing in their traditional lifestyle within their families and clans was not only the natural thing to do, but would also prevent the loss of identity. To that end, 1999 finds the Lumbee living in much the same way they have for over 500 years—close to their family, extended family, neighbors, and friends; attending school and church in their local communities; and maintaining their independence while demanding their rightful place in positions of leadership and authority in their home land.

Robeson County is the largest of the 100 counties in North Carolina, though this distinction is based on geography and not population figures. The county is located in the southeastern part of the state, and its geography and environment are unique. In Robeson County, the piedmont region and the coastal plains area meet, which means that the land is diverse and contains rich farmlands, creeks, branches, and swamps. The flat land of Robeson is used for farming, the county's major industry. The Lumber River winds through the county and flows through neighboring Hoke and Scotland Counties in North Carolina and empties into the Pee Dee River in South Carolina, which is 12 miles from the Pembroke city limits. Located geographically in the western end of Robeson, Pembroke is known as the economic, cultural, and educational center of the Lumbee Tribe, who are descended from the Cheraw and other Siouan-speaking people who have inhabited the area since the beginning of the area's recorded history. The Lumbee have always been an industrious people and have contributed greatly to the success and progress, economically and educationally, of not only the Pembroke area, but the county and state as well.

The corporate limits of Pembroke are located in the center of several un-incorporated communities—Union Chapel, Evans Crossing, Hope Well, Prospect, Mt. Airy, and Deep Branch—where the majority of the population is Lumbee. From these communities outside the town limits come the people from the Lumbee nation who have made lasting contributions to the town. Traditionally, Lumbees are clannish, and their history shows a cohesiveness that is based on community, family, extended family, church, and school. Though there are very definite differences in the people from these rural communities, there is an attachment from community to community due to family ties and the clannish nature of the Lumbee. It is understood in Lumbee country that we are all connected to each other, if not by genealogy, than by a common bond of caring for each other, which has developed over the centuries as a form of extended family life. The Lumbee are segregated by the communities they live in, but they do this by choice, and it has been a very successful movement that has resulted in the Lumbee remaining a distinct and separate race of people in the midst of an otherwise homogeneous population.

A study by the Lumber River Council of Governments states that there are more than 30,000 people living within a 7-mile radius of the corporate limits of the town of Pembroke. Statistics show that more than 90 percent of the population in this 7-mile radius are Native American. The study does not include the students, faculty, and staff of the University of North Carolina, which is also located inside the corporate limits of the town.

Members of the Lumbee nation have contributed to the church, incorporating into their lifestyle the beliefs and principles expressed in the King James version of the Bible soon after European contact. They have established and maintained connections with the National and State Southern Baptist Convention and the United Methodist Conference (locally, statewide, and nationally) and have displayed leadership in a smaller way in the Church of God, the Assemblies of God, and the Pentecostal Holiness Church.

In 1900, the Lumber River Holiness Methodist Conference was organized under the leadership of several members of the Lowry family of the Hope Well area. In addition, the Burnt Swamp Baptist Association, which is an affiliate of the North Carolina State Southern Baptist Convention, was started as early as 1881. The Southern Baptist is the major Christian church of the Lumbee, with 61 churches belonging to the local association.

The Native Americans of Robeson County lived in peace and harmony with their non-Indian neighbors from the first European settlement in the 1700s until the State of North Carolina began to legislatively disenfranchise them. For more than 100 years, the Lumbee enjoyed the same rights and privileges as the whites in the area. Serving beside their white neighbors, they fought in the Revolutionary War, as well as the War of 1812. Political and economic conditions changed for the whites in the area, and, in 1835, the State of North Carolina amended its constitution to deny non-whites the right to bear arms, to vote, to own property, and to attend white schools. For a period in North Carolina history, Native Americans were not allowed to learn. This was a dark period in Lumbee history and resulted in 50 years of illiteracy, ignorance, and no opportunities for formal education. The Reconstruction Act of 1898 restored citizenship to the Lumbee but did not restore the right to attend white schools. There were no organized schools for Native Americans, and the Lumbee refused to attend the inadequate schools attended by African-American children in the area.

Until 1885, the Lumbee were simply called "Indians." But, in 1885, the North Carolina General Assembly passed a bill that named the Native Americans in Robeson County "Croatans." Hamilton McMillan of Red Springs decided that the Native Americans in the area were descendants of John White's "Lost Colony" and introduced the legislation in an attempt to strengthen his personal theory on the Lumbee. This act, more importantly, also established separate schools for the Native Americans.

The Lumbee were renamed by the State of North Carolina in 1911. Legislatively, they became the "Indians of Robeson County." In 1913, the State of North Carolina again changed the name to the "Cherokee Indians of Robeson County," and finally, in 1953, in a joint resolution, the House and Senate of North Carolina passed a local referendum changing the name to "Lumbee," which was voted into law by the Lumbee themselves. The name, of course, is derived directly from the Lumbee River, which is the Native American designation of the Lumber River.

The University of North Carolina at Pembroke (UNCP)

The University of North Carolina at Pembroke, steeped in rich Native American history, is located within the corporate limits of Pembroke. The post-secondary institution has endured just about as many name changes as the Native American community that surrounds it. It began as an "all-Indian" school and was, in the beginning, for the "Indians of Robeson County" only.

In 1887, the Honorable Hamilton McMillan, member of the North Carolina House of Representatives from Robeson County, pressed for legislation establishing a Normal School for the "Indians of Robeson County." This Normal School was the equivalent of a high school, with graduation achieved after the junior year. Following graduation from the Normal School, students were allowed to teach in the local school system. Education beyond graduation from the Normal School was not required for teachers. The legislation stipulated that Native American students enrolling must be 15 years of age and must sign a contract agreeing to teach school in Robeson County for one year as part of the criteria for attending the Normal School. This act also appropriated $500 from the state treasury for salaries. The law stated that a building must be provided by the community, and the funds could not be used for anything other than salaries. If these funds were used for anything other than salaries, the legislature of 1889 would repeal the 1887 act.

The act further named the trustees of the first school for Native Americans. They were W.L. Moore, James Oxendine, James Dial Sr., and Preston Locklear, and their responsibility was to carry out the provisions of the act. Under the authority of the legislature, these gentlemen appointed three additional trustees: J.J. Oxendine, James Brayboy, and Ollen Oxendine. These Native American trustees were charged with the duty of establishing a Normal School.

The trustees purchased an acre of land at Pates, opposite the New Hope Church, and supervised the construction of a two-story building. This location was 1 mile west of the present site of the university. W.L. Moore was elected as the first principal and teacher. There were 15 students enrolled in 1887. Because the trustees had met the criteria of establishing a Normal School as required by the 1887 legislation, $1,000 was appropriated for the school in 1889. This appropriation remained the same for several years after that.

In 1909, the trustees selected a new site in Pembroke. The land was purchased and the legislature that year appropriated $3,000 for a new building. As the years passed, more high school courses were offered, including vocational training for boys and girls. In 1921, Judge L.R. Varsar of Lumberton sponsored a bill in the North Carolina Legislature which appropriated $75,000 for the erection of a modern building. Old Main, the first brick structure, was built in 1922. It contained an auditorium which would seat 700 people, offices for several departments, and classrooms for business, foreign languages, English, philosophy and religion, social sciences, and education. The State of North Carolina granted the institution a high school standard rating in 1924.

Although the legislature created a Normal School in 1887, the actual schoolwork at the Normal level did not begin until the fall of 1926. In the interim period, instruction was at the elementary and secondary levels. Classes in Normal work began in the fall of 1926, and the first Normal class graduated in June 1927. That same year, the state board of education gave the school a standard high school rating. In 1929, two years of college work were added to the high school curriculum, and a new home economics building was erected.

In 1935, a school for the teaching of the deaf was organized; it was operated for three years and then was discontinued. A full-time librarian was added to the teaching staff in 1938, and in June of that year, the first three-year college diplomas were awarded.

In the fall of 1939, the high school was separated from the college and was moved to a new building on a separate site, off the campus. This historic site has been preserved and is located beside the campus of UNCP. This move allowed for the expansion of the faculty for the college and the addition of the senior year to the college curriculum. In 1940, the first degrees were awarded to members of the four-year college class.

The name of the present UNCP has changed through the years. It was established in 1887 as the Croatan Normal School. The legislature, on March 8, 1911, changed the name to the Indian Normal School of Robeson County. In 1913, the name was again changed by the legislature to the Cherokee Indian Normal School of Robeson County, and in 1941, the legislature again changed the name to Pembroke State College for Indians. This was the only state-supported four-year college for Native Americans in the nation and maintained that distinction until 1953. In 1949 "for Indians" was legislatively dropped from the name, and the school became Pembroke State College. In 1969, the legislature again changed the name, and the college became a regional school, Pembroke State University. In 1973, the legislature moved again, and they established the 16-campus system of the University of North Carolina, and Pembroke State became one of the 16 institutions. In 1996, the campus with probably more name changes than any other institution in the nation became, officially, the University of North Carolina at Pembroke.

From its establishment until 1945, the enrollment of UNCP was limited to the "Indians of Robeson County." In 1945, the admission policy was extended to include persons from other federally recognized Native American tribes. In 1953, the General Assembly again amended the statutes to allow the board of trustees to extend the admissions policy. They decided to allow the board of trustees to admit "any other persons of the Indian or white races who may be approved by the Board of Trustees." Acting under this authority, the board of trustees agreed in May 1953 to approve the admission of white students.

A native of Pembroke and a Lumbee, Dr. Joseph Oxendine now serves as chancellor of UNCP and has held that position since 1989. He is only the second Native American to hold that position. The first was Dr. English E. Jones, who served as president from 1962 until 1972, as the chancellor of Pembroke State University from 1972 to 1979, and as chancellor emeritus from 1989 until his death.

The board of trustees is comprised of 13 members, five of whom are Lumbee. They are Sybil L. Collins, who will serve until 2001; McDuffie Cummings, whose term expires in 1999; Cheryl R. Locklear, who will serve until 1999; Gervais Oxendine, who will serve until 2001; and Roger Oxendine, who will serve until 1999.

One

Local Faces

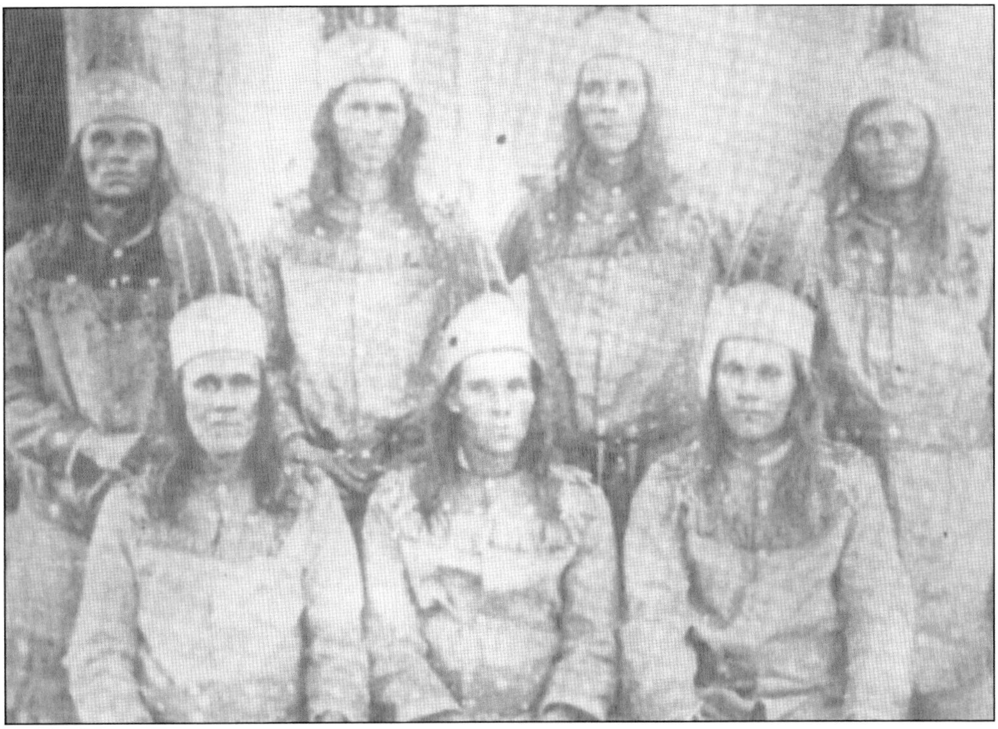

In the early 1900s, several fraternal organizations comprised of Native American leaders were established in the Prospect, Magnolia, Pembroke, Saddletree, Oxendine, and Union Chapel communities. Known either as the Confederation of Red Man's Lodge or the Tecumseh Lodge, the groups were dedicated to protecting Native Americans and maintaining social order. Although the majority of the functions and ceremonies of the lodges were not known to the general population, each Native American community had its own organization. It is told by the elders that one of the purposes of the lodges was to protect the Native American blood line by discouraging any dating or marriage between Native Americans and non-Native Americans. This photo is of the Red Man's Lodge, which met upstairs at the Antioch School. Shown here c. 1914, from left to right, are as follows: (front row) Abner Chavis and his sons, Bunyan Chavis and William (Bill) Chavis; (back row) Jordan Chavis, Governor Chavis, George Washington (Wash) Bell, and Leander Chavis.

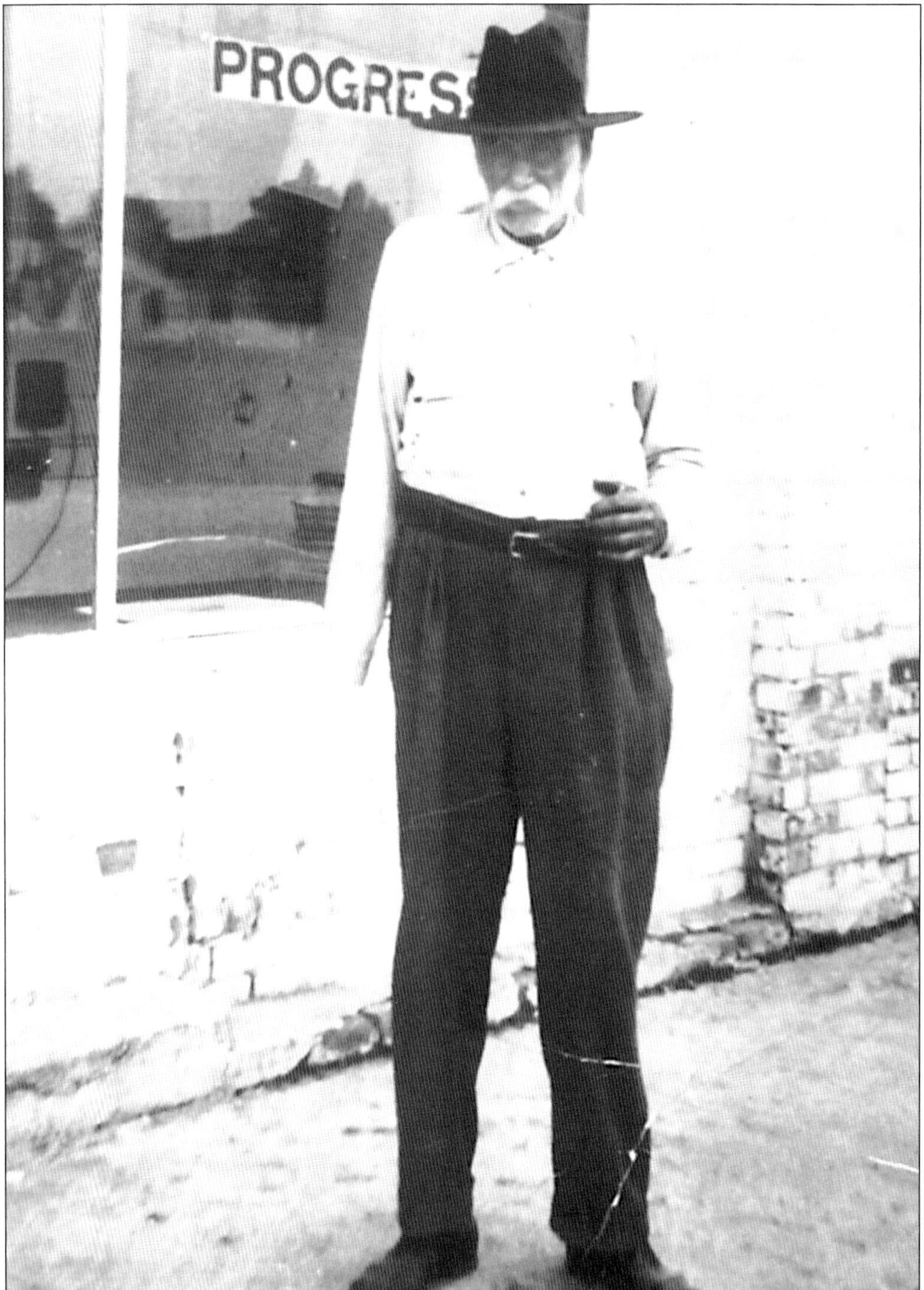

Born on May 17, 1874, Herbert Lowry served as the chief of police for the town of Pembroke and was on the Pembroke police force for 30 years. Referred to as "one-armed Herbert," he was greatly respected by the citizens of the town. Lowry died on April 12, 1964. He is shown here in downtown Pembroke in 1947.

Billy Lowry was born in 1860 and died in 1961. He raised his family on the property of what is now the University of North Carolina at Pembroke and eventually sold some of his land to the university.

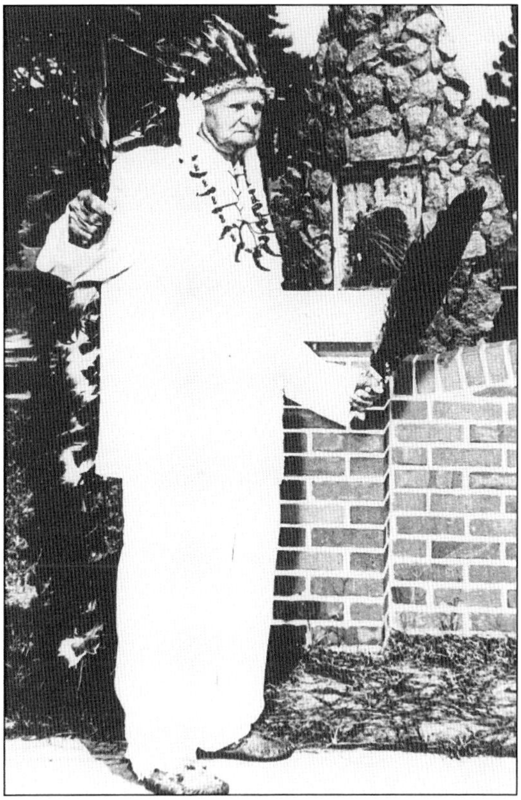

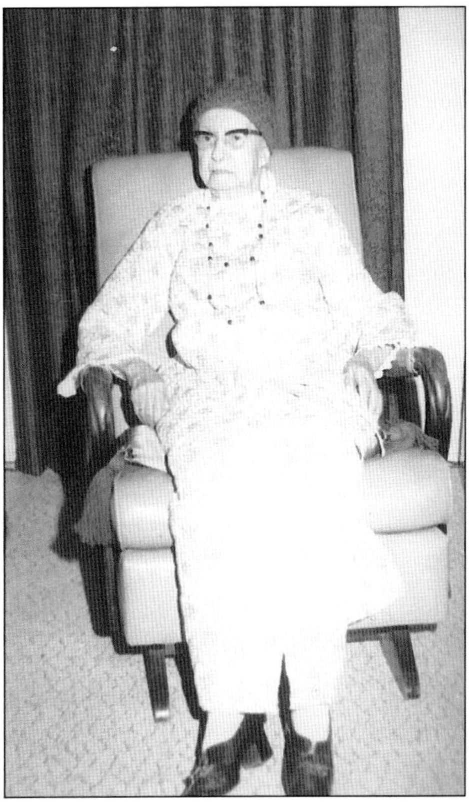

Mrs. Nancy Revels lived to be over a century old. She was the daughter of Calvin Lowry, brother of Henry Berry Lowrie.

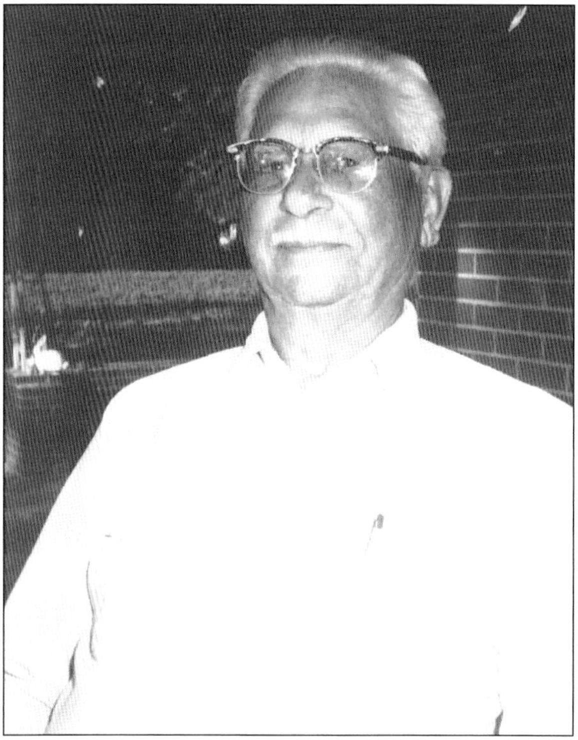

Mr. Claude Lowry was known for many years as an elder who could and would retell the history of the Lumbee people. He was born in 1911 and died in 1992. Mr. Lowry was one of the first graduates of Pembroke Normal School.

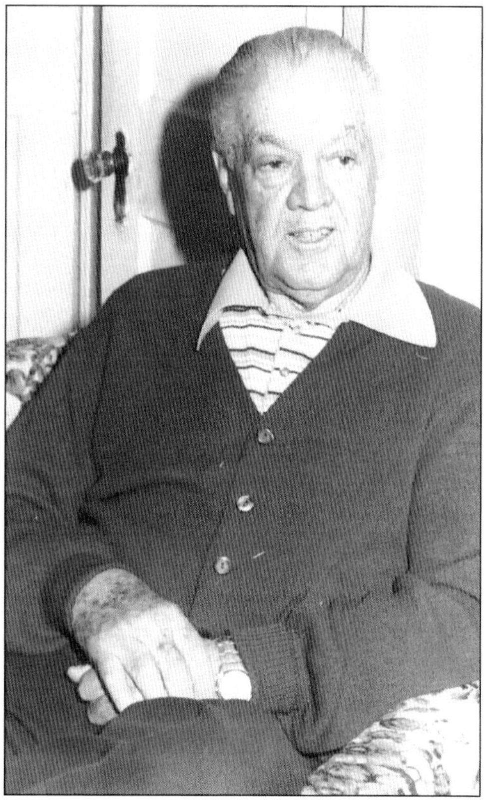

Dr. Earl Lowry was the son of Rev. D.F. Lowry. He is a medical doctor and served as a surgeon to several presidents. He is the first Lumbee to hold the distinction of being the private physician to a president of the United States.

Ira Pate Lowry was a longtime band director at PSU. He and his wife, Reba, owned the *Pembroke Progressive*, which operated from June 19, 1947 (the maiden issue), until at least May 1956, though it is true that only the first two years the paper was on microfilm.

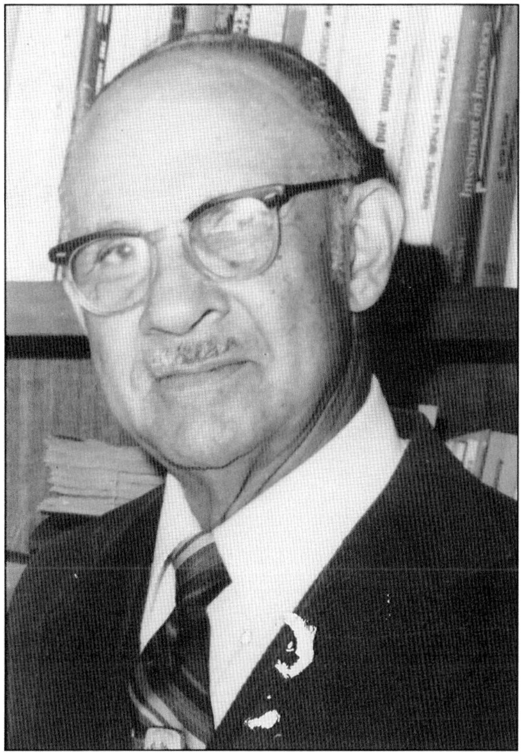

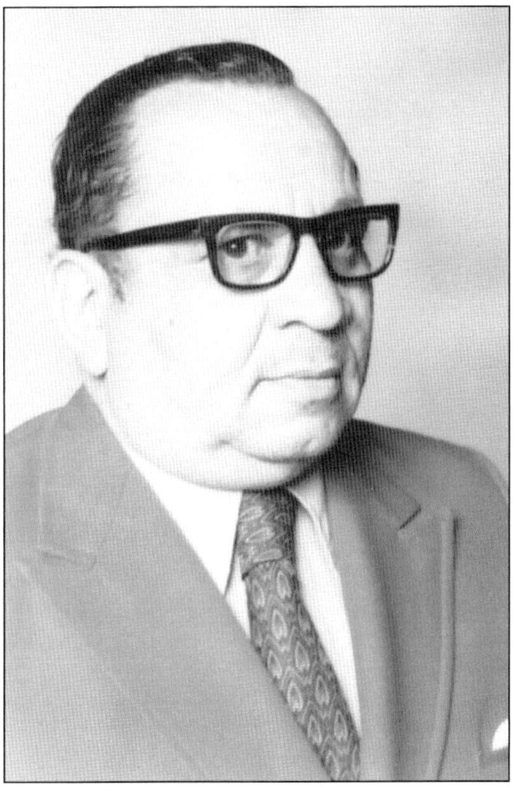

Bernard Lowry was a Pembroke businessman, a retired schoolteacher, principal, farmer, and magistrate. He owned many buildings in Pembroke and operated a vast rental property business. Lowry also operated the College Exxon for many years. Born on July 21, 1912, he was the son of the late Abner and Rose Lowry. He was the ninth of 16 children and was married to the former Lillie Mae Strickland. Mr. Lowry was proud to tell people he "belonged to the Hopewell Lowrys." He was active with the Boy Scouts Organization and the Pembroke Kiwanis Club, in which he held the position of president and lieutenant governor. He died on February 16, 1997.

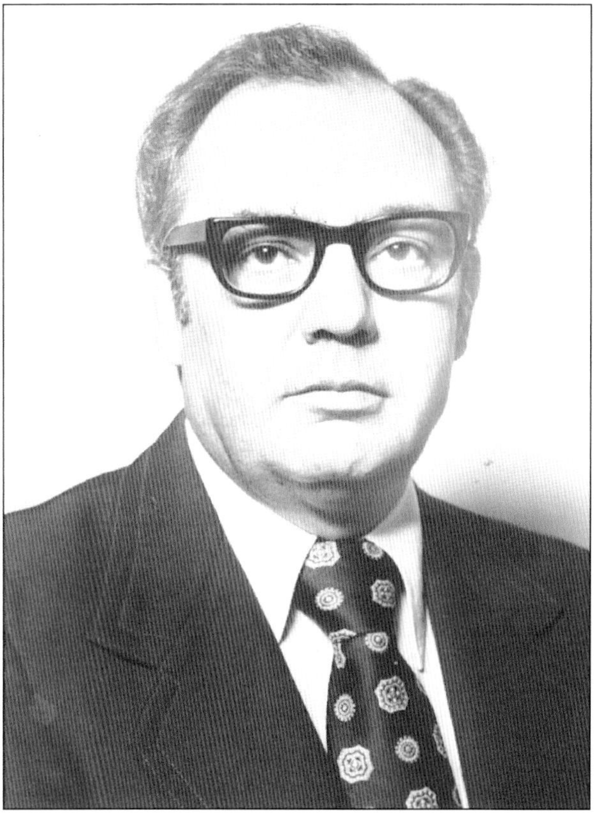

Herman Dial, a member of the Prospect community, was the first Native American to serve as chairman of the Robeson County Board of Commissioners. He was elected to the Robeson County Board of Commissioners in 1970 and served for 16 years. In the beginning of his political career, he was the only Native American serving on that commission. He also operated Dial's Insurance Agency in Pembroke. His son, Carlton Dial, continues to operate that business. Dial was born on May 28, 1928, and died on March 20, 1990.

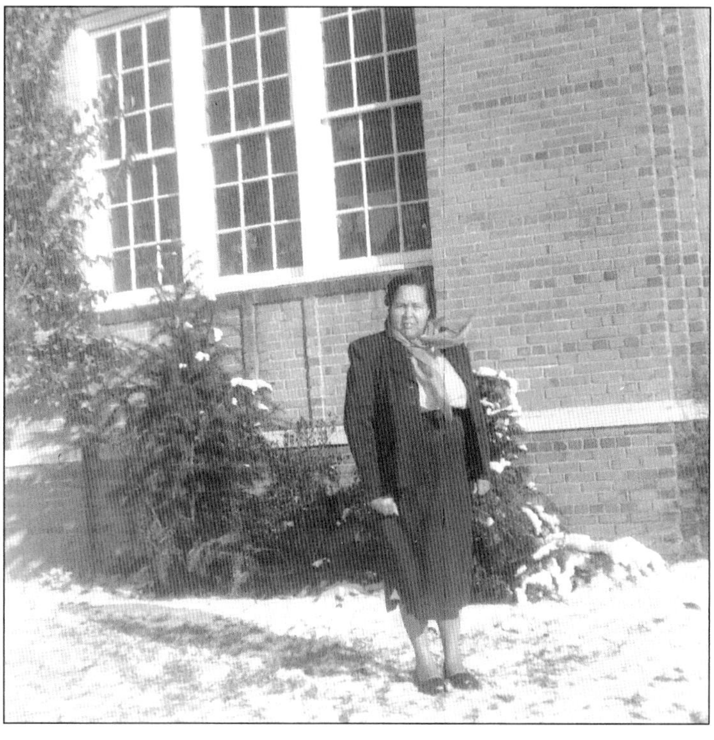

Mrs. Dial, or "Miss Ruby," as the students affectionately called her, is shown attending to business at the Pembroke High School Library despite the weather in this 1960 photo. Mrs. Dial died in 1979.

Allen G. Dial was elected to the Pembroke Town Council in 1997. He owns and operates Dial's Auction Company, is a real estate broker, and owns Lumbee Drive Inn, as well as rental property.

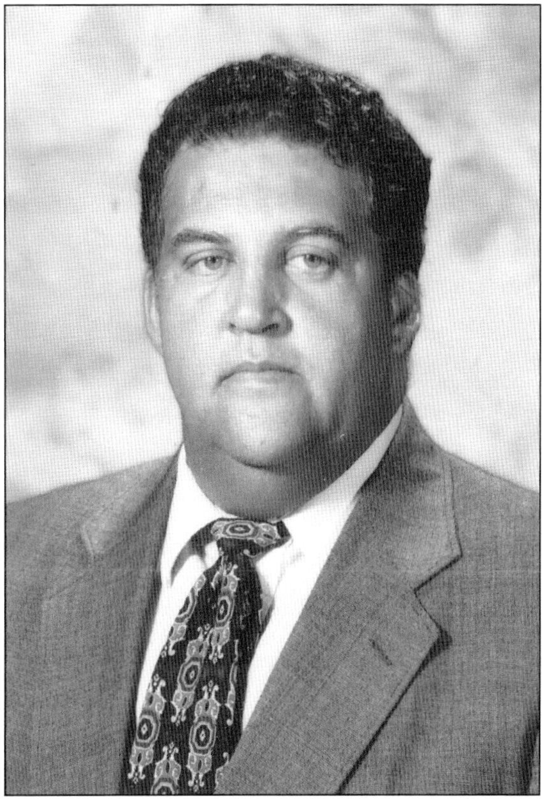

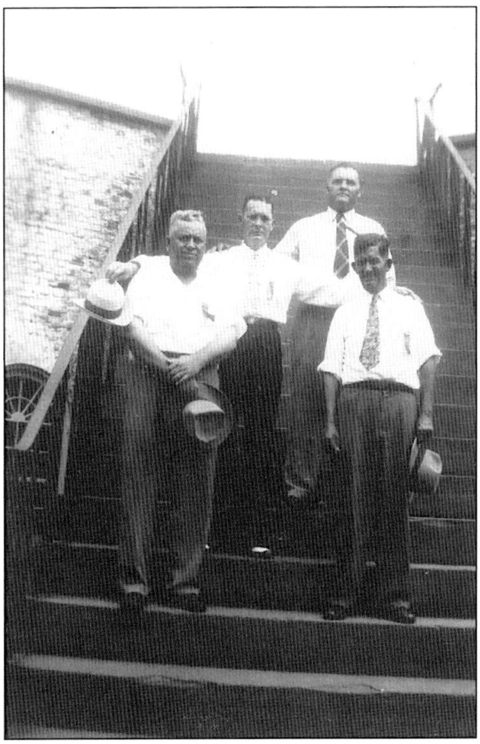

Mr. A.G. Dial, shown top rear, attended a Firemen's Convention in Washington, D.C. in the early 1950s.

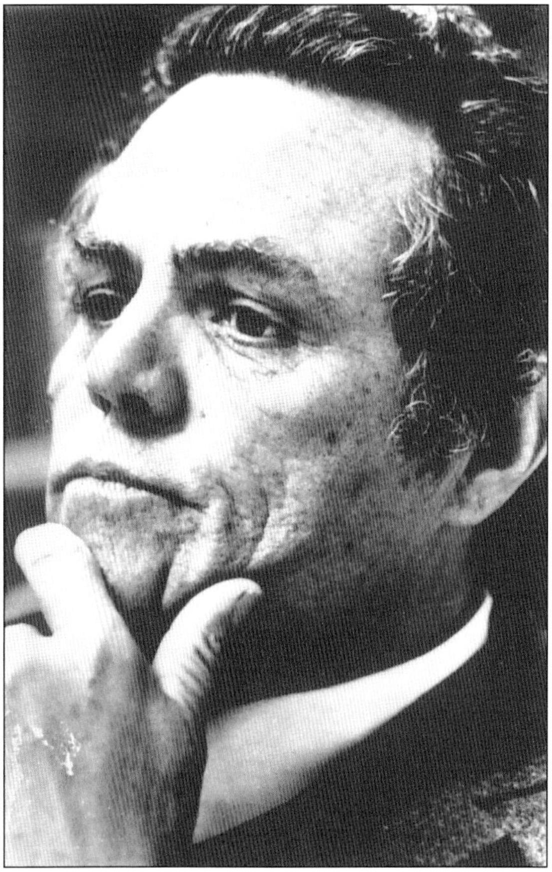

Dr. Adolph Dial was a Pembroke businessman, civic leader, and historian. Dial established the Indian Studies Department at Pembroke State University and served as the first chairman of that department. He had vast business holdings in the town of Pembroke, including Colony Plaza Shopping Center, the shopping center that houses the Piggly Wiggly, the North Carolina State Credit Union, and Jones Family store. He was a major stockholder in the Lumbee Bank and served for two terms in the North Carolina House of Representatives in 1986–1990. He was author of several books on Lumbee history, including *Lumbee*, and he co-authored *The Only Land I Know*.

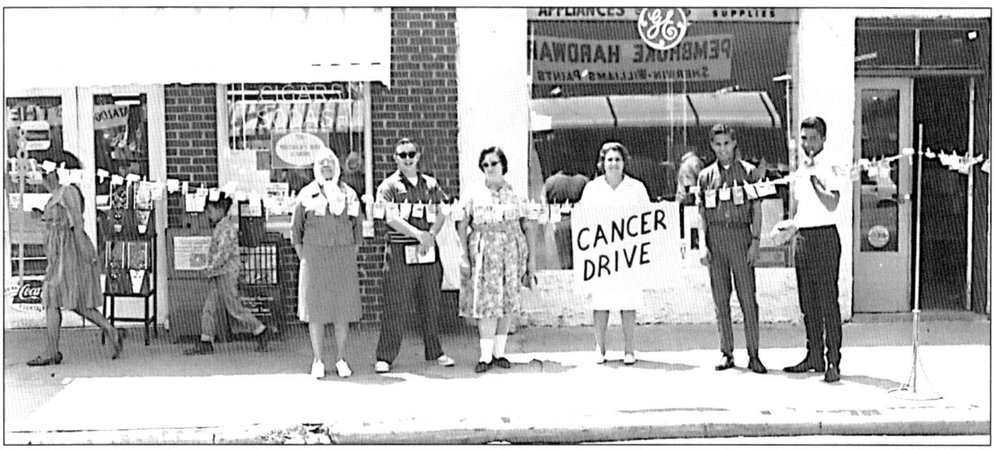

Mrs. Edna Lee Oxendine, a well-loved schoolteacher, also headed the Cancer Drive each year in Pembroke. She served as the chairperson of the Cancer Drive for 15 years and is shown here (wearing the scarf) at a cancer drive during the 1950s. Once a year she would hang a clothesline on the street in downtown Pembroke, and people would pin their donation for the Cancer Drive to it. Mrs. Oxendine was also a well-respected and admired elementary schoolteacher until her retirement.

Hilton Oxendine was the first Native American to join Pembroke State University's Chancellor's Club. He was also the first Native American to have a Toyota franchise, which he operated in the city of Lumberton for several years. Hilton and his brother, Hubert Oxendine, were also the first Native Americans to own and operate a restaurant—the Old Foundry Restaurant on West Fifth Street—in the city limits of Lumberton. Hilton Oxendine was also the first Native American to serve on the Lumberton City Council.

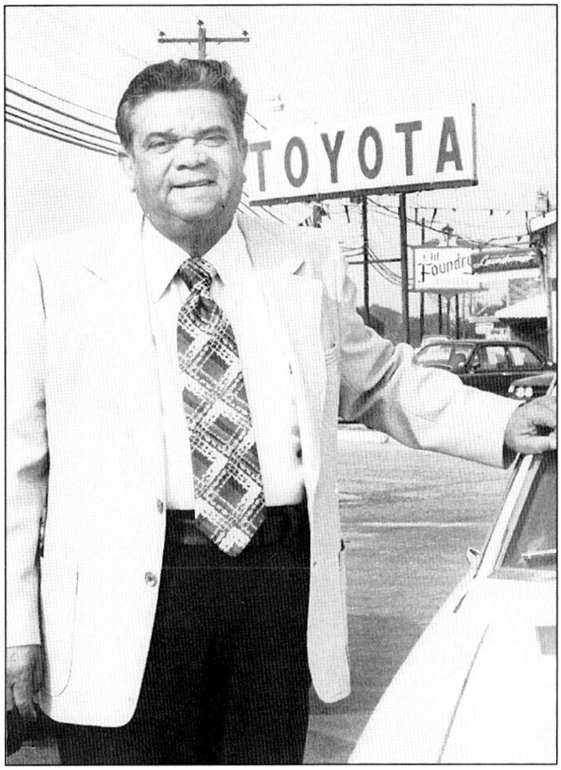

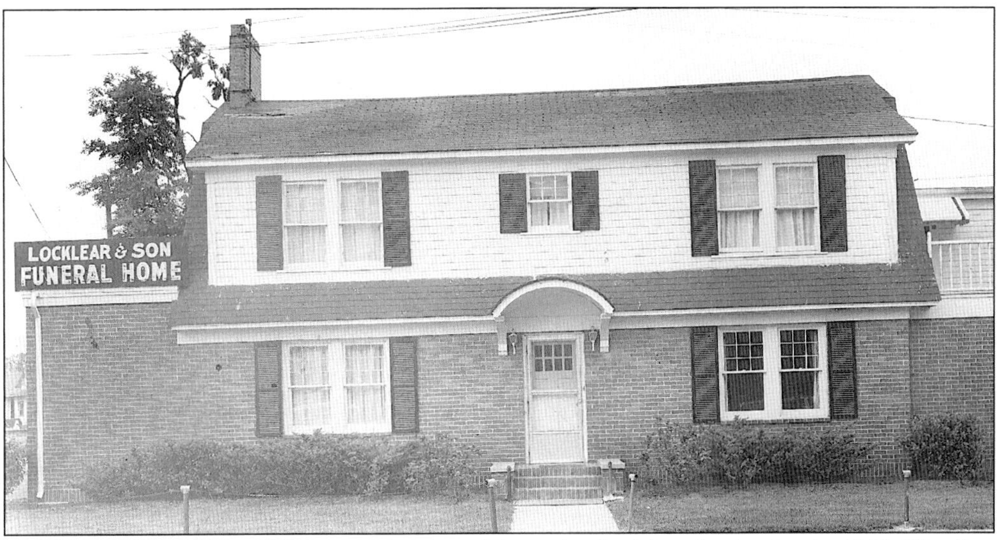

Locklear and Son Funeral Home was operated from this building, beginning in 1948. The first Indian-owned funeral home was owned and operated by Mr. Luther Locklear. He and his wife, Pattie, and family resided upstairs and operated the funeral home in the downstairs portion of the building. Locklear and Son celebrated 50 years of service to the community in 1998 and is now operated by Samuel Locklear, the son of Luther and Pattie. He has moved the business to a spacious building on the Union Chapel Road. Lumbee River Legal Services, Inc. now operates from this building. It is now called the Julian T. Pierce Law Building. Samuel Locklear also served as mayor of the Town of Pembroke from May 1961 until April 1963.

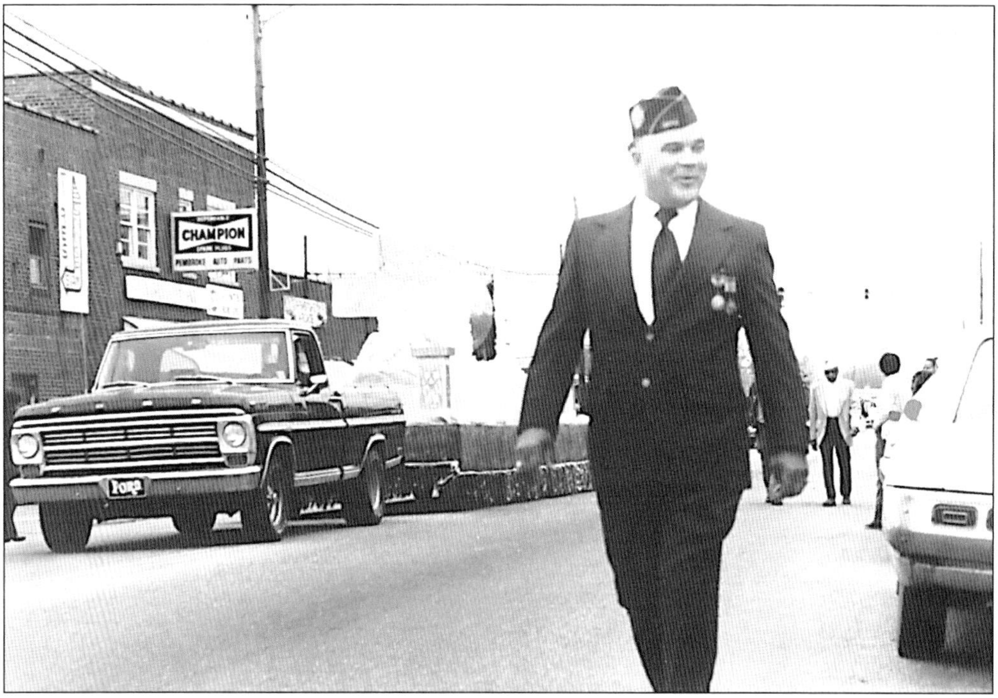

Simeon Oxendine, the son of the late James C. "Sonny" Oxendine, is shown during a Veteran's Day Parade in 1973. Oxendine was a World War II veteran and a member of the Pembroke Veterans of Foreign Wars. He gained national attention at the 1958 Ku Klux Klan rally in Maxton when he and Shelton Woriax were pictured in *Life Magazine* displaying the Klan flag. Oxendine owned Pembroke Service Center and served on the Robeson County Board of Education for a number of years. He died in 1988 at the age of 69.

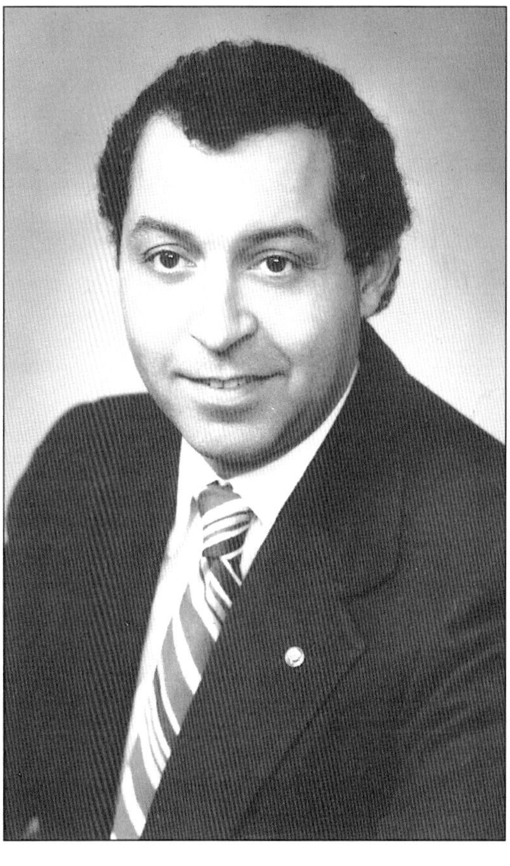

Horace Locklear was the first Lumbee to be admitted to the North Carolina Bar. He opened his office for the practice of law in 1972 in Lumberton, across from the Robeson County Courthouse. Locklear was one of the incorporators of the Lumbee Regional Development Association, Inc. in 1968. This nonprofit agency continues to serve the Lumbee people with services through federal, state, and local grants. Locklear was elected to the North Carolina House of Representatives in 1977 and served until 1983. He is a native of the Saddletree community.

Gene Locklear is a native of the Mt. Airy community and was the first Lumbee to be recruited into the major leagues. Shown here in his Padres uniform, he was an outfielder for the Cincinnati Reds, the San Diego Padres, and the New York Yankees. He played professional baseball for several years before retiring to concentrate on his art career.

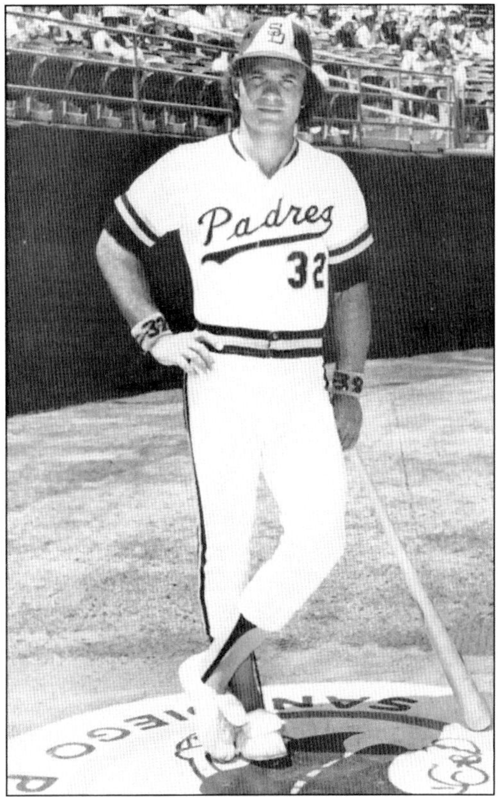

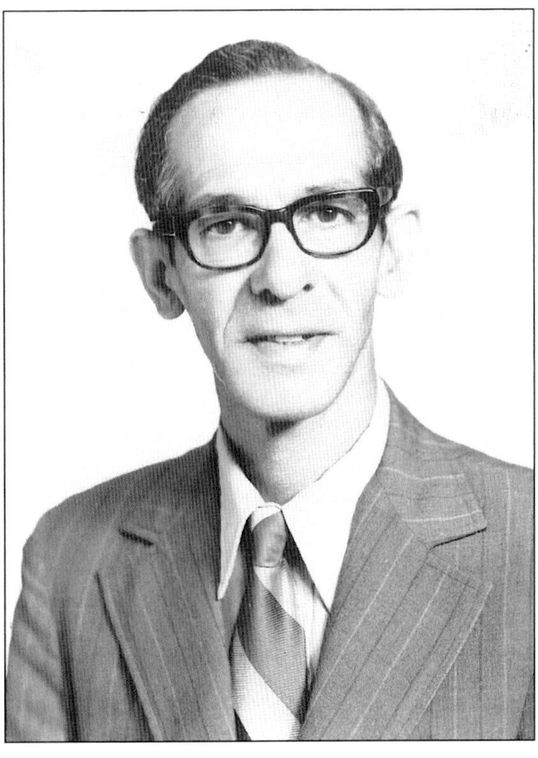

Elmer W. Hunt was the first Lumbee professional photographer. He was also a schoolteacher at Magnolia School for many years, and was the first Native American photographer at Pembroke State College.

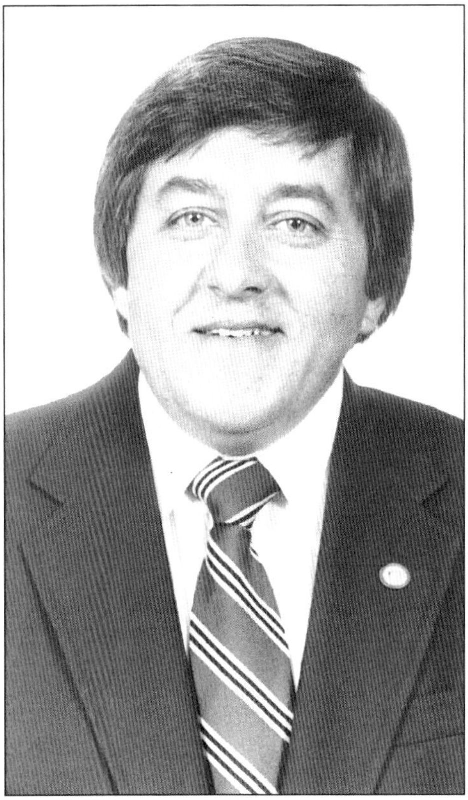

Mayor Milton Hunt has been the mayor of Pembroke since December 1983. He owns and operates Hunt's Drywall, and he is presently serving as the chairman of the Robeson County Democratic Party.

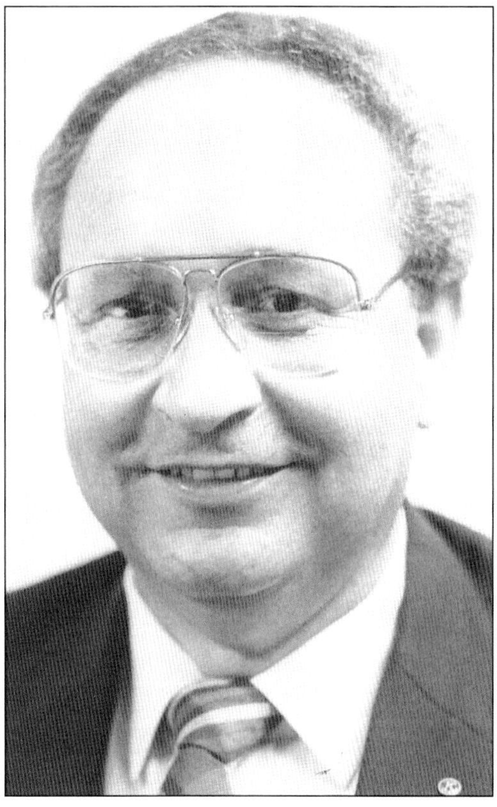

Reggle Strickland served as mayor of the Town of Pembroke from December 1975 until November 1979. One of the housing developments of Pembroke Housing Authority, Strickland Heights, is named in his honor.

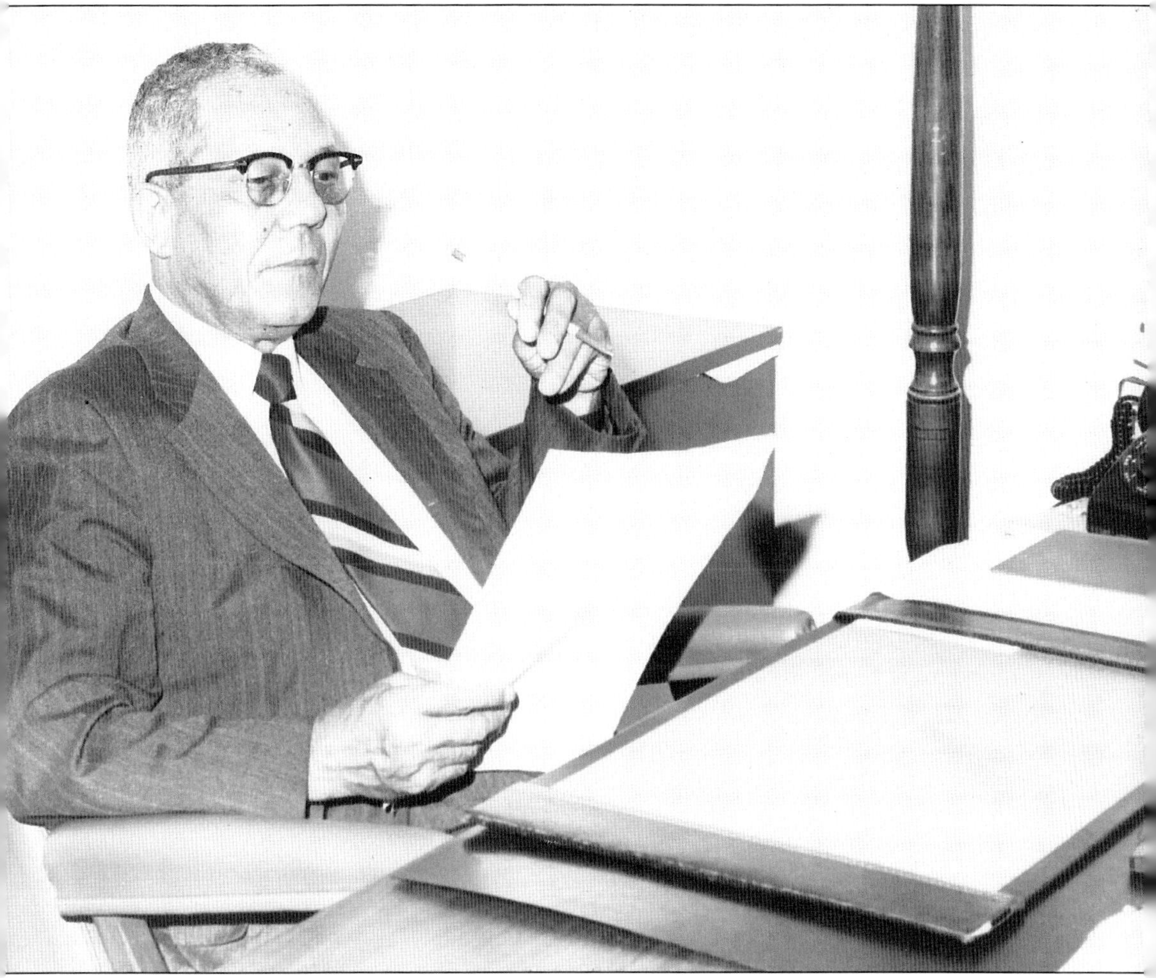

John L. Carter served as the secretary of the Burnt Swamp Baptist Association from 1939 until 1978. He was a lifelong member of Mt. Airy Baptist Church, where he served as the Sunday school superintendent, deacon, secretary, and treasurer for many years. He was the registrar at Pembroke State College and served in that capacity for 15 years, from 1959 to 1974. Prior to his employment with the college, Carter served as the principal of Green Grove School from 1929 to 1930 and taught at Pembroke High School from 1954 to 1959. Carter also served for 18 years as the secretary of the university's board of trustees. In addition, he served on the board of trustees of Robeson Community College for many years.

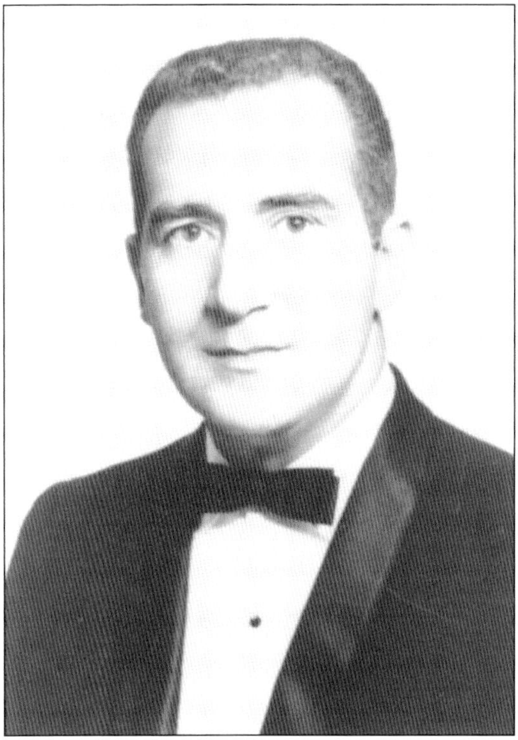

John Mark Brooks was the first Native American to serve as chairman of the Robeson County Democratic Party. He was the principal at Magnolia School at the time of his death in 1983. He was also the first Native American to serve on the Board of Directors of Southeastern Regional Medical Center in nearby Lumberton, North Carolina, the only hospital in the county.

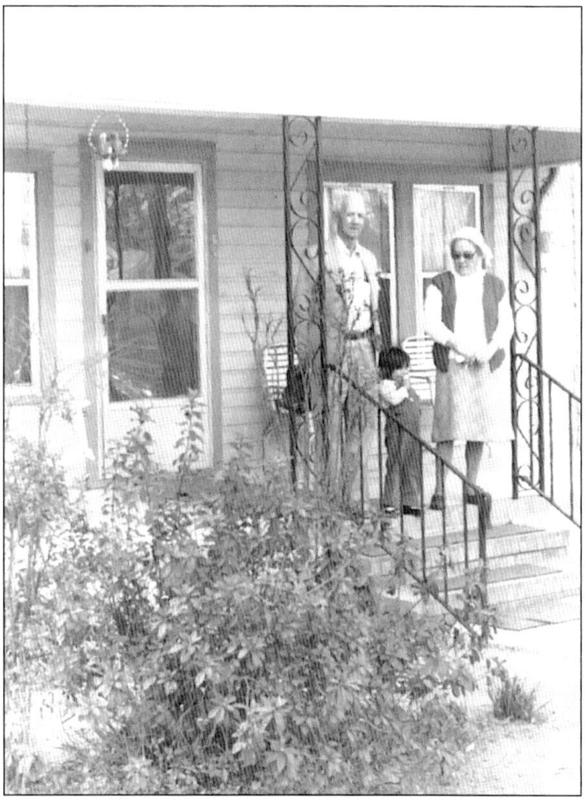

Mr. and Mrs. Clayton Bell are shown here on the front porch of their Pembroke home. They operated City Cafe from 1950 until 1955. Later, they became vendors at Bell's Produce. Mr. Bell died in 1986, and Mrs. Bell in 1987.

Klynt Deese was locally known as the "Mule Skinner." He was severely injured in an automobile accident when he was in the sixth grade. He owned and operated Deese's Music Store in Pembroke for several years.

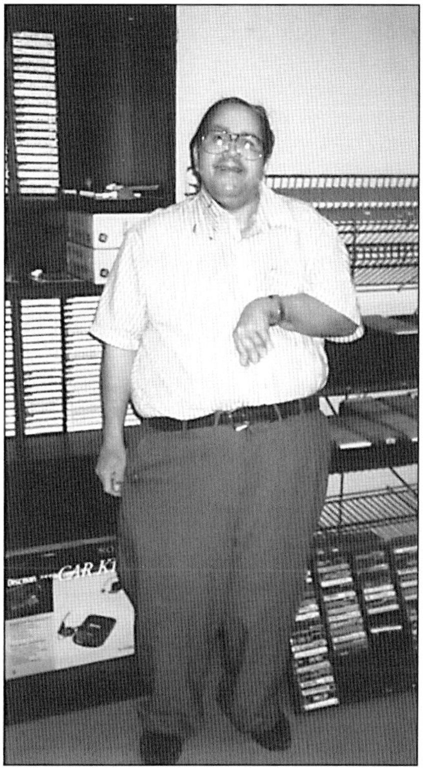

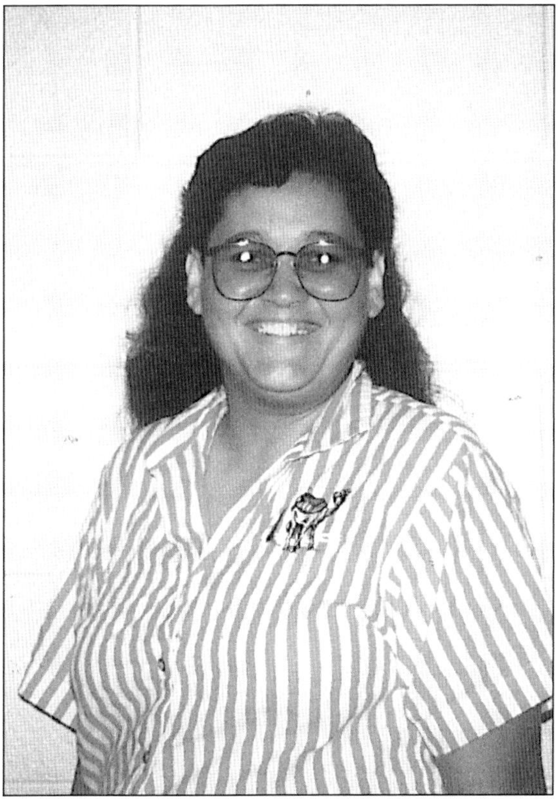

Patricia Brayboy resides in the Hopewell community, directly behind the Henry Berry Lowrie birthplace. She is the first Lumbee to be hired by the American Red Cross. In 1998, she became the first Lumbee to be the director of the Robeson County Chapter of the American Red Cross.

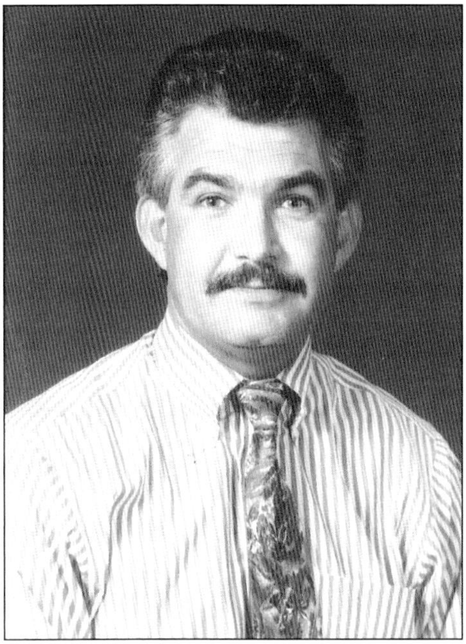

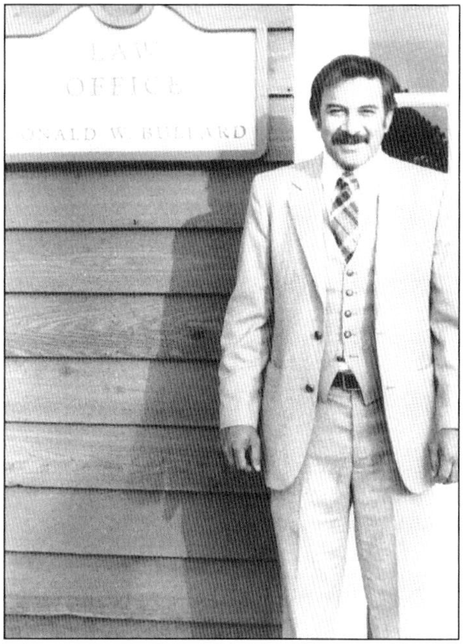

Left: Charles Gregory Cummings is the economic developer for Robeson County. A Pembroke businessman, he operates CG's Convenience Store, a car wash, and other local businesses. He has served on the town council and has held his position since 1990. He is the first Lumbee to be hired as economic developer for the county, and he began in that position in 1996. *Right:* Donald Bullard is shown in 1974 when he began his legal practice in the town. His office is located on the Union Chapel Road, as is the law office of Ron Sutton, the representative for District 85 in the North Carolina General Assembly. Bullard is one of several Lumbee attorneys in the town.

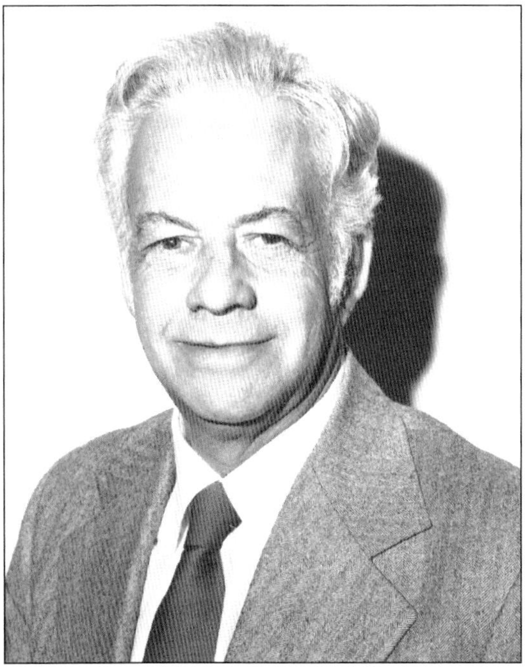

Tommie Dial was the first Lumbee to test for the North Carolina State Bar Exam. He was not admitted to the practice of law in the State because there were no provisions for minority attorneys in the state. He served the community in several capacities, among them executive director of Lumbee Regional Development Association. Dial is author of *The Indian Credo*, which details the discrimination of Lumbees and their determination that causes them to rise to positions of power and authority, in spite of obstacles and oppression.

Mr. Lloyd Brewington and his wife, Viola, operated Viola's Grill on the Union Chapel Road in Pembroke for many years. He is shown in 1973 surrounded by a gigantic head of collards that he grew in his home garden.

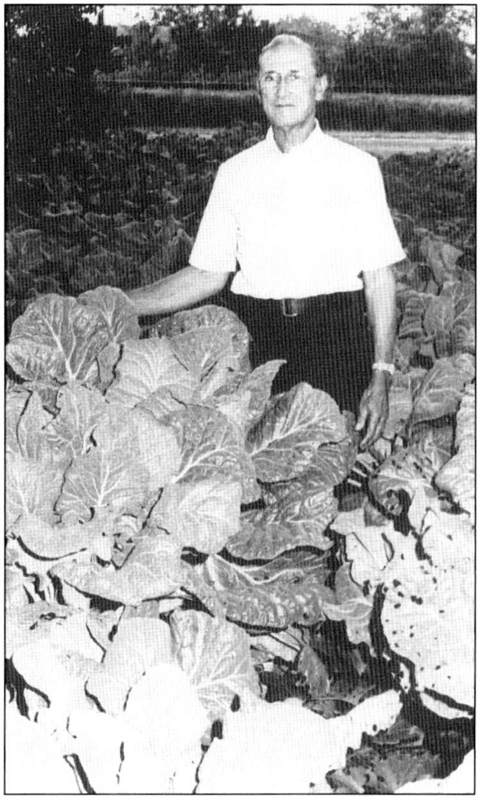

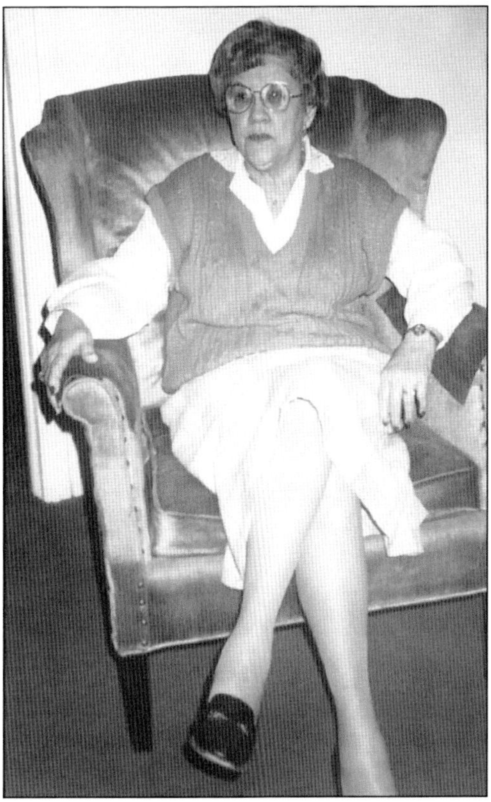

Mrs. Evelyn Cummings worked in the Pembroke Post Office for many years. The first female Native American employed there, she is now retired.

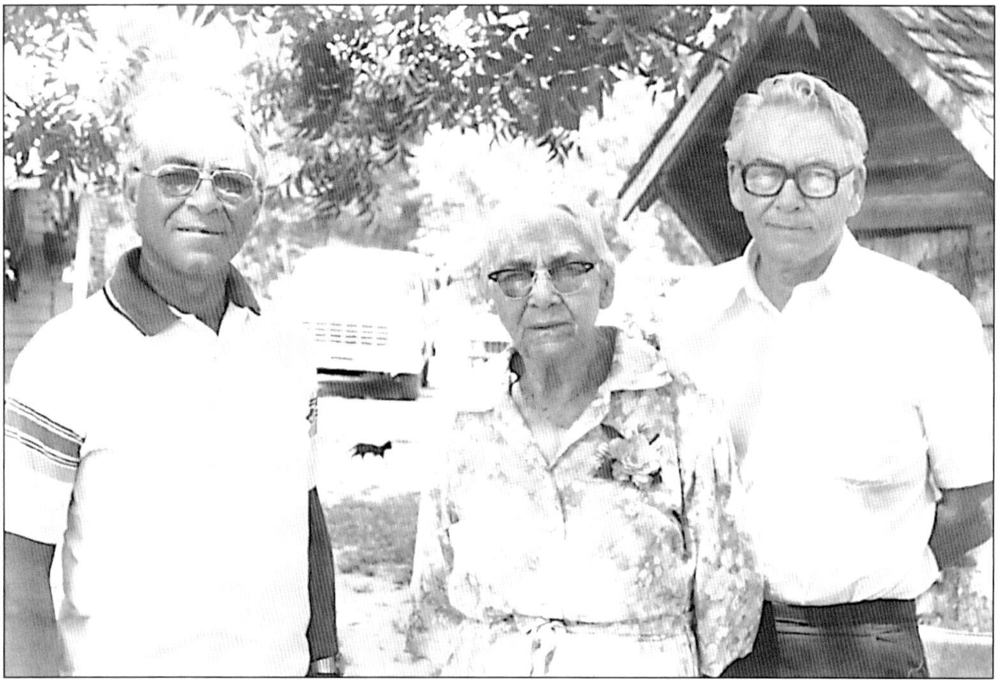

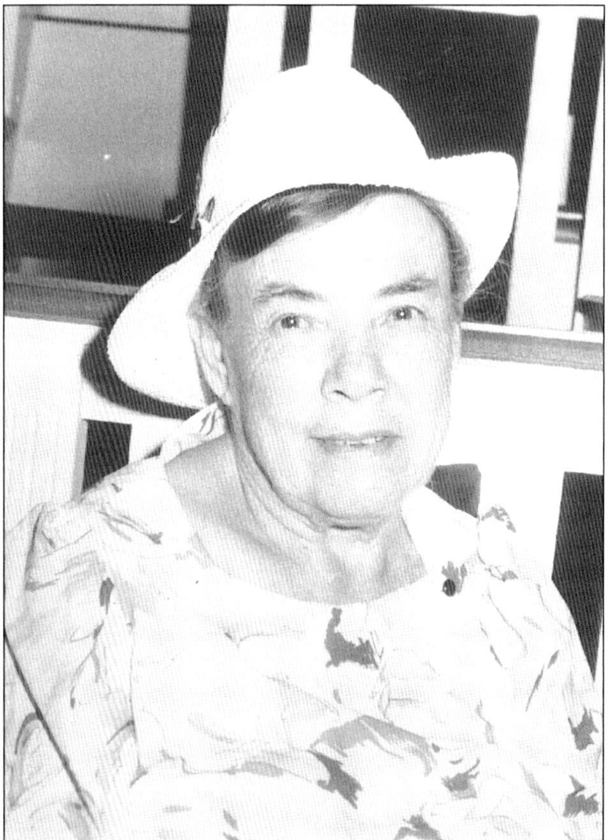

Mrs. Lennie Lowry, the wife of James Clennie, is shown here with her two sons, Monroe Lowry (owner of Pembroke Electric) and Curt Locklear (owner of Pembroke Hardware).

Dicy Ann Sampson operated the Dairy Queen in Pembroke for more than 25 years. She was born in 1909 and died in 1993. Her son is Rev. Kelly Sanderson, a Baptist minister who pastors Mt. Olive Baptist Church in the Saddletree community.

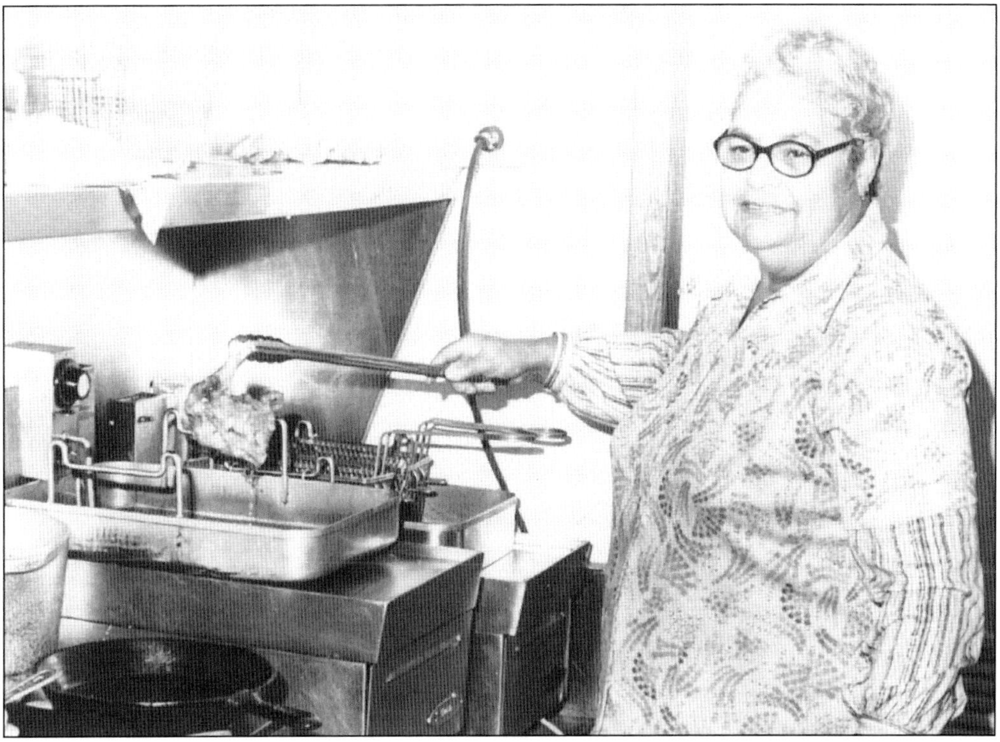

Marcella Bullard is shown here in the kitchen of the cafe she operated at Pates Stockyard for several years. She was married to the late Harvey Bullard, who was a member of the Pembroke Police Department for many years.

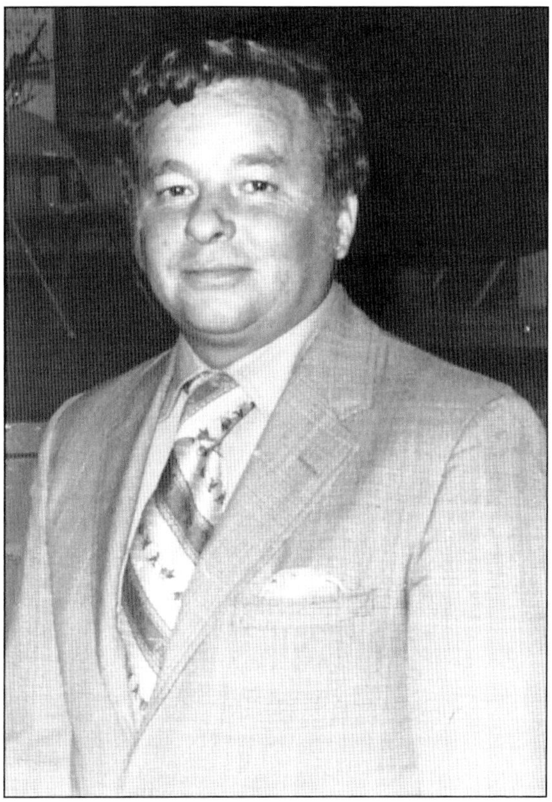

Juddie Revels Jr. served as mayor of the town of Pembroke from 1973 until 1975. He is the owner and operator of Revels Funeral Home, following the tradition of his father, Juddie A. Revels Sr., who began Revels Funeral Home in Pembroke. Revels Funeral Home was the second funeral home owned and operated by Native Americans in the community.

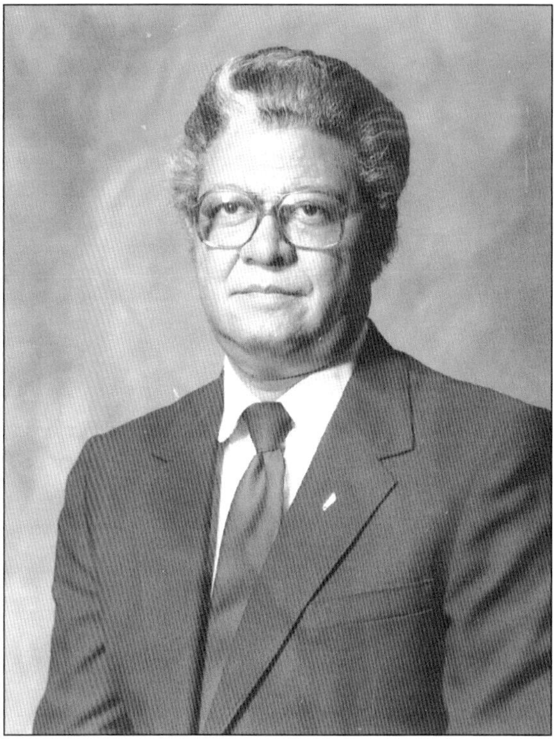

James A. "Pete" Jacobs served as the mayor of the town of Pembroke from 1979 until 1983. He retired as tax supervisor for the county of Robeson in 1996, having been the first and only Native American to hold that position.

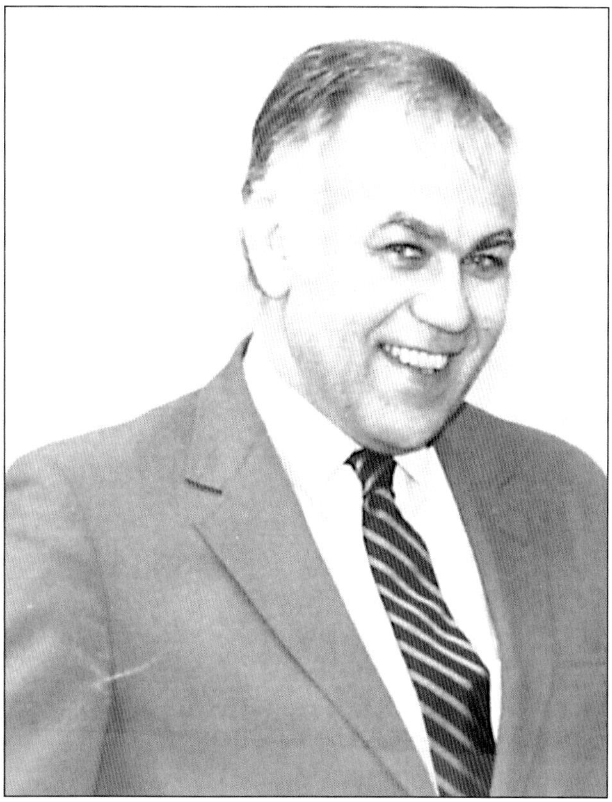

Purnell Swett was the first Native American to serve as superintendent of the Robeson County School System. Following merger, he served as superintendent of the public schools of Robeson County until his retirement in 1998.

Dexter Brooks was the first Native American to serve as a superior court judge in Robeson County. He is currently the senior resident superior court judge for Robeson County.

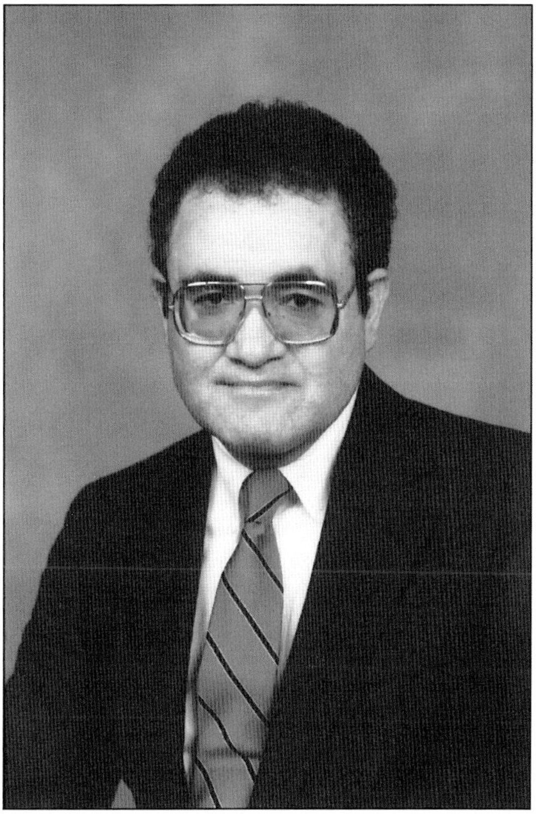

Foy and Hildeth "Bloss" Cummings were outstanding lay leaders in the Baptist Association. Their son, Rev. Mike Cummings, serves as director of missions for the Burnt Swamp Baptist Association and was recently elected as vice president of the North Carolina State Convention.

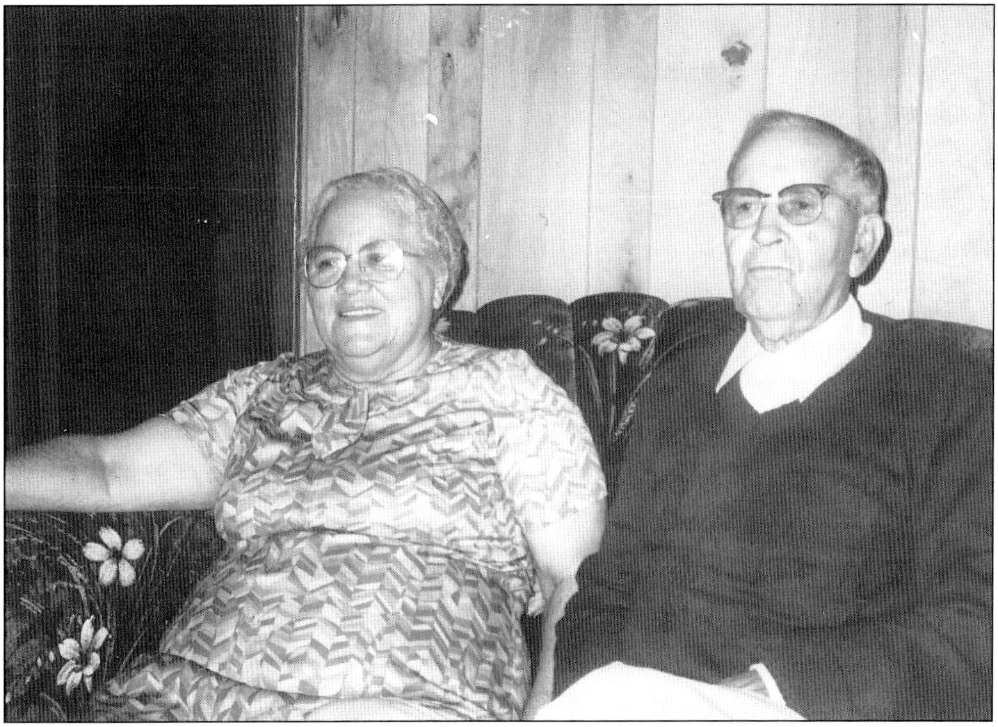

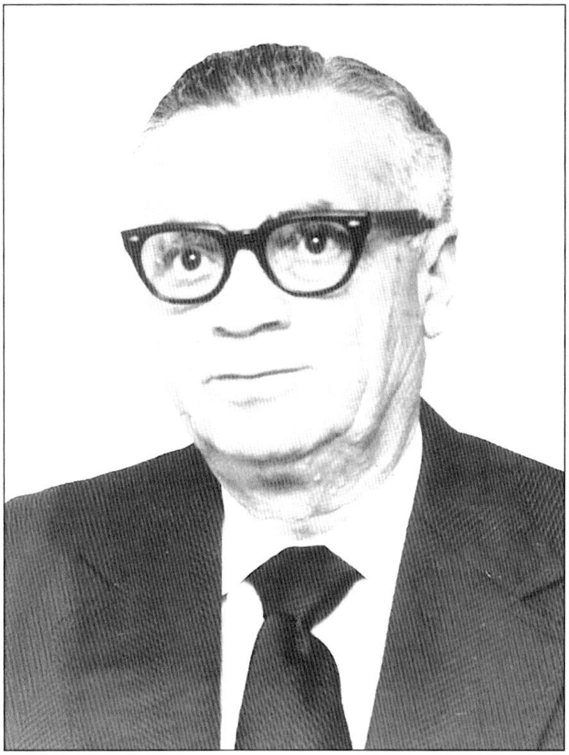

Pembroke businessman Harry West Locklear was the first Native American to serve on the Robeson County Board of Education. He was also the business manager for the Indian Fair, which came to Robeson County for several years.

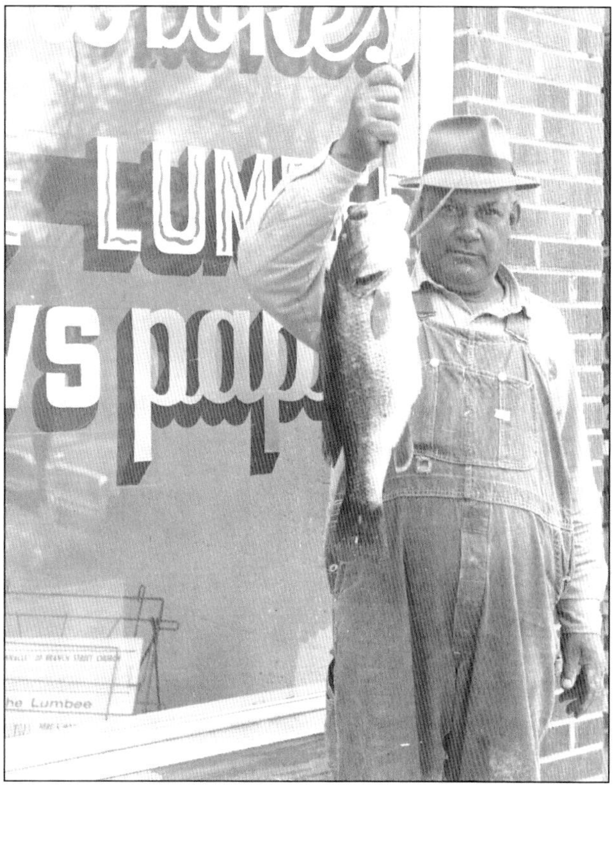

Archie Locklear of Route 1 Maxton shows off a proud catch from a 1967 fishing trip. He caught the 5.5-pound bass at the Lumbee Recreation Center (now the North Carolina Indian Cultural Center).

Two

PLACES OF WORSHIP AND RELIGIOUS LEADERS

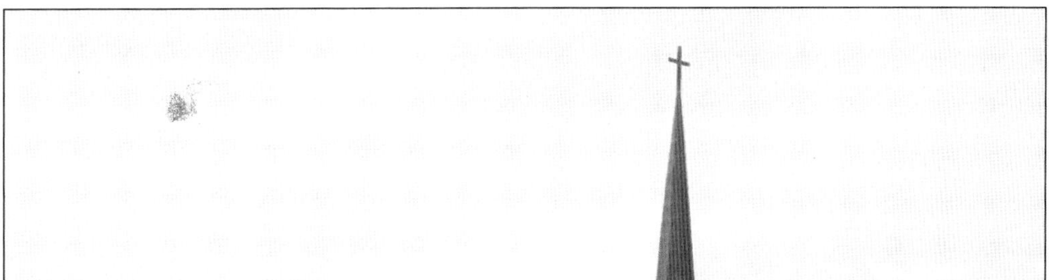

This is a view of Harper's Ferry Baptist Church, one of the many Baptist churches in the area.

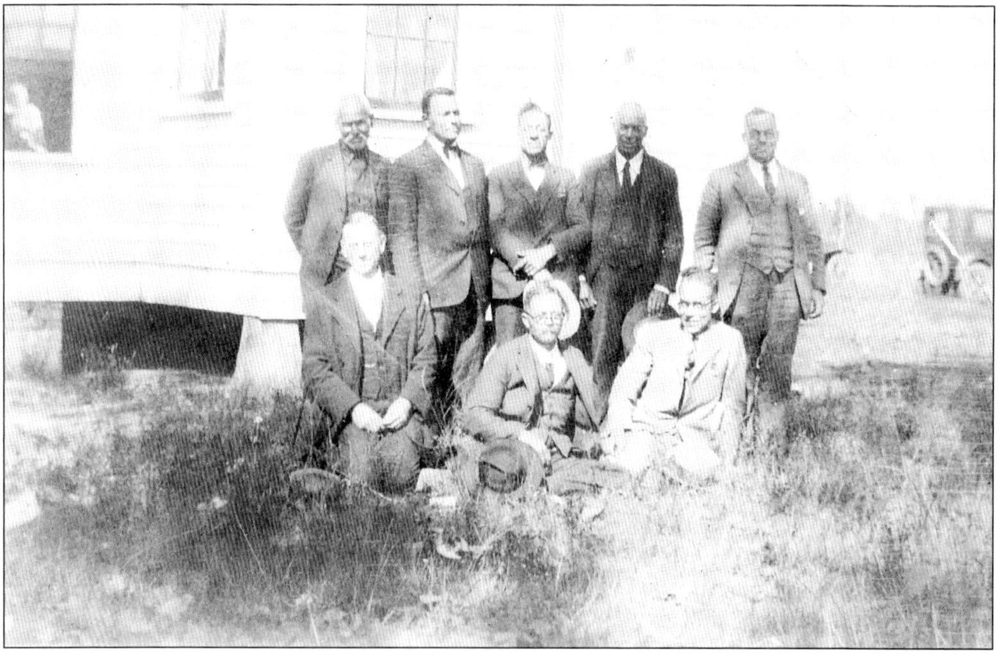

A group of Native American ministers is shown on the site of the first orphanage facility for Native Americans. This facility became a part of the North Carolina Baptist Children's Homes and became known as the Odum Home.

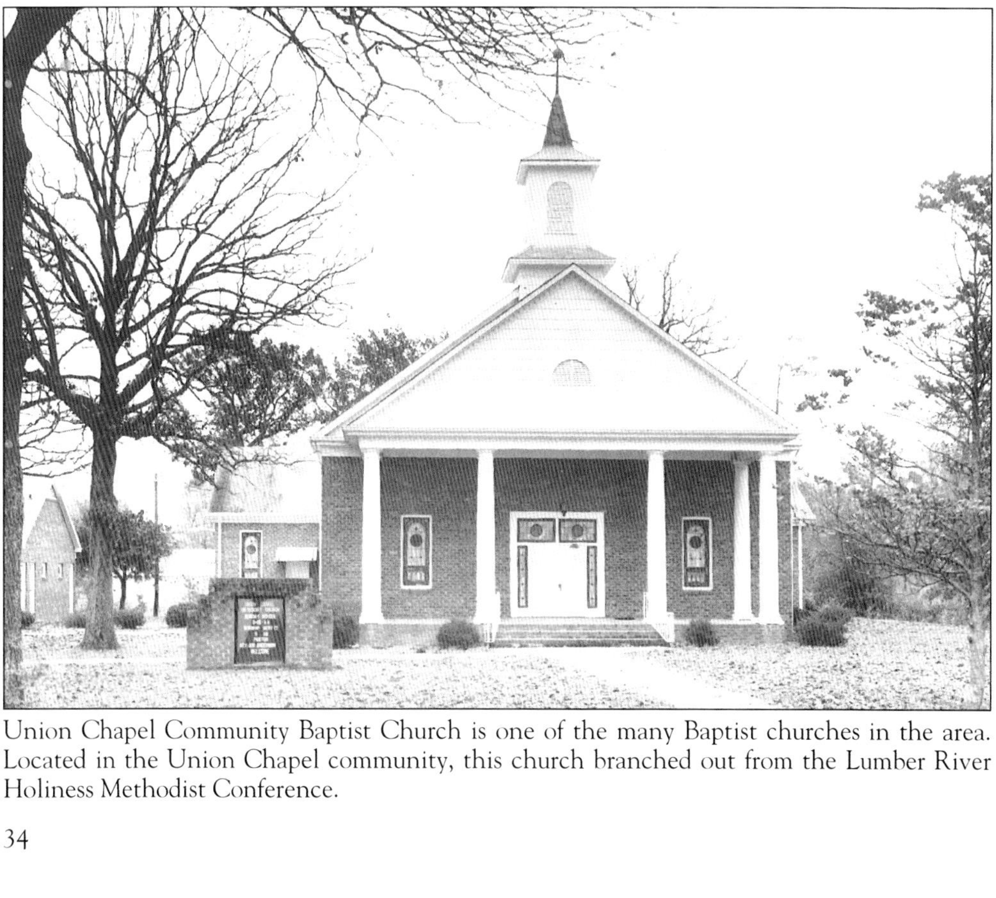

Union Chapel Community Baptist Church is one of the many Baptist churches in the area. Located in the Union Chapel community, this church branched out from the Lumber River Holiness Methodist Conference.

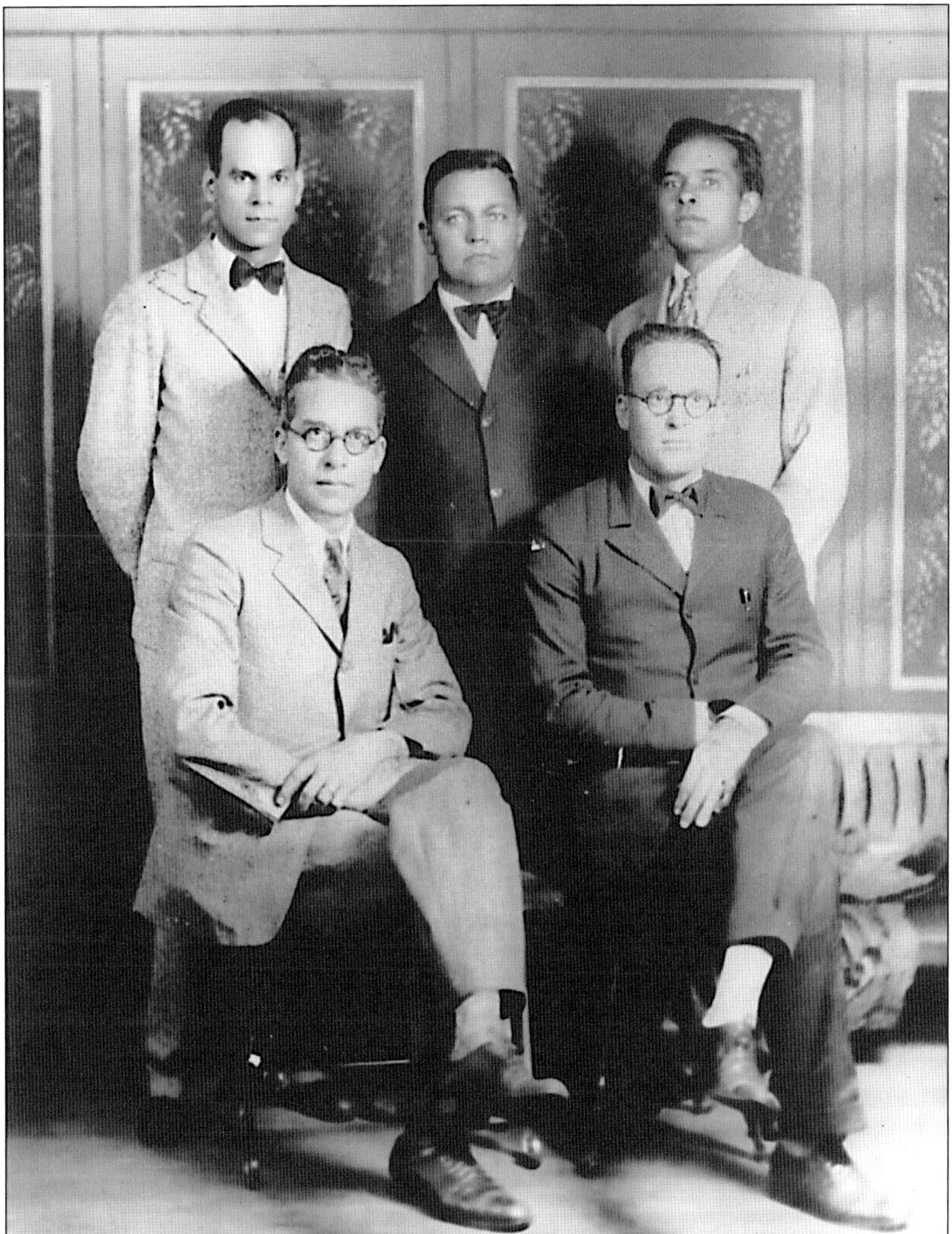

These members of the Burnt Swamp Baptist Association attended the annual meeting of the North Carolina Baptist State Convention held in Raleigh in 1930 to petition for membership. At this convention, the association was granted an associate membership. Attending the convention were, from left to right, L.W. Jacobs, Bill Locklear, Tom Oxendine, C.E. Locklear, and Gaston Revels.

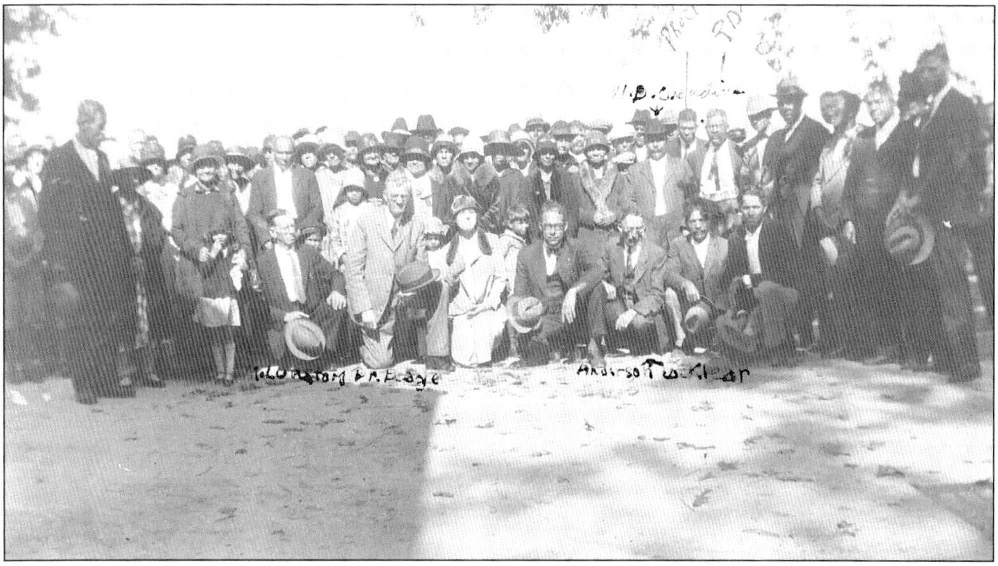

The 1929 annual meeting of the Burnt Swamp Baptist Association was attended by representatives from the North Carolina Baptist State Convention. The association had petitioned to become a member of the state convention; the group officially became a member in 1930. State representatives included Dr. J.W. Beagle; Dr. Maddry, executive secretary of the state convention; Dr. Livingston Johnson; Dr. Skyler; and Reverend Pridgen.

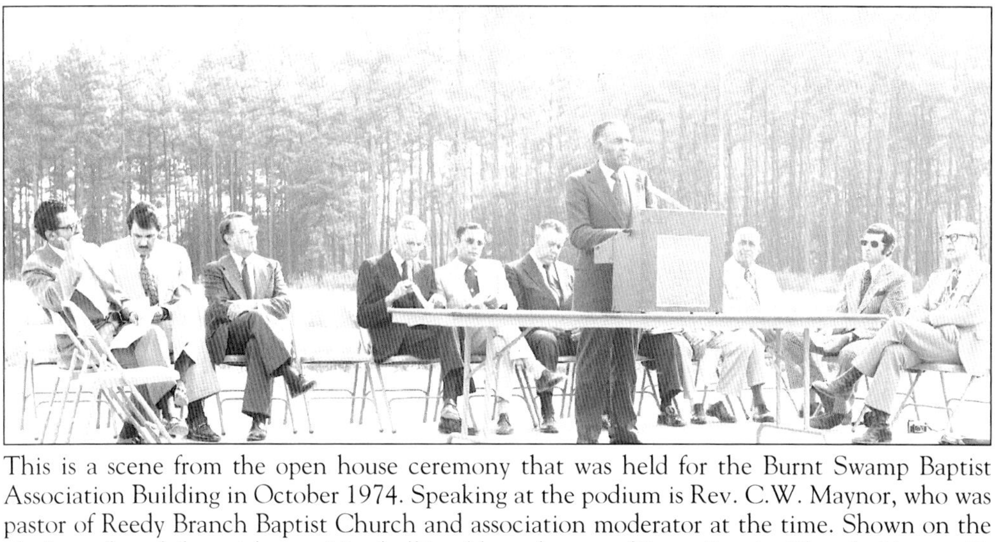

This is a scene from the open house ceremony that was held for the Burnt Swamp Baptist Association Building in October 1974. Speaking at the podium is Rev. C.W. Maynor, who was pastor of Reedy Branch Baptist Church and association moderator at the time. Shown on the platform, from left to right, are Marshall Locklear, deacon of Berea Baptist Church; Tommy D. Swett of Harper's Ferry Baptist Church; Rev. Roger Williams of Kinston, director of Eastern North Carolina Children's Homes; Rev. King Maynor, pastor of Mt. Elim Baptist Church; Rev. R.W. Maynor, pastor of Oak Grove and Piney Grove Baptist Churches; Rev. Sanford Locklear, pastor of New Point Baptist Church; Rev. Tony Brewington, director of missions for the Burnt Swamp Baptist Association; and Rev. Joe Watterson, director of chaplain work for the Baptist State Convention.

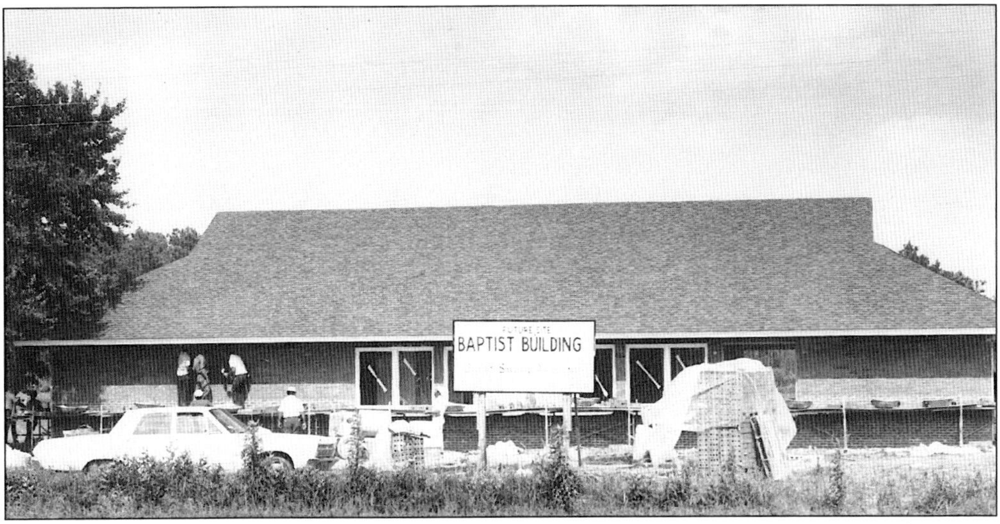

Construction on the Burnt Swamp Baptist Association Building is seen here. Later, the name of the building was shortened to "the Baptist Building." The facility houses the offices for the director of missions, his secretary, and a community ministry program.

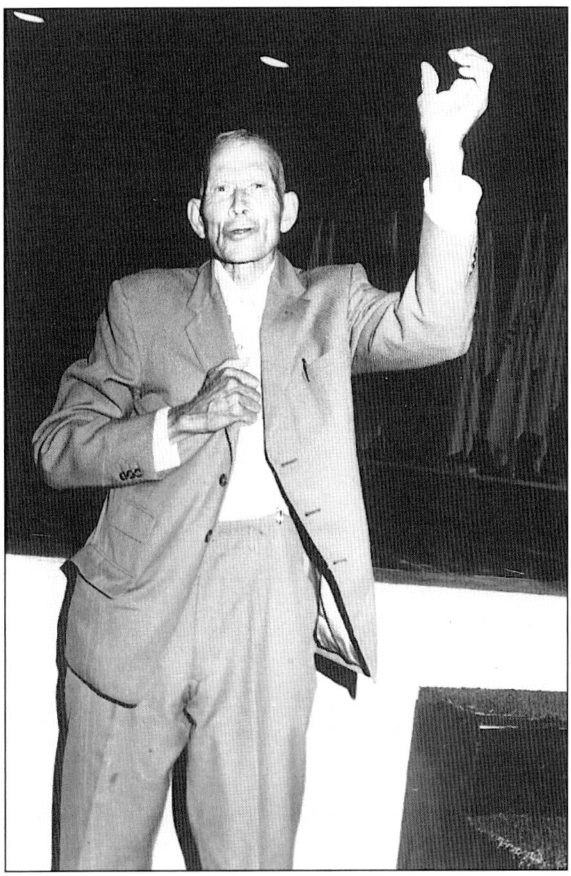

Mr. Proctor Locklear is shown at the centennial celebration of the Burnt Swamp Baptist Association in 1980. He was 89 years of age at the time.

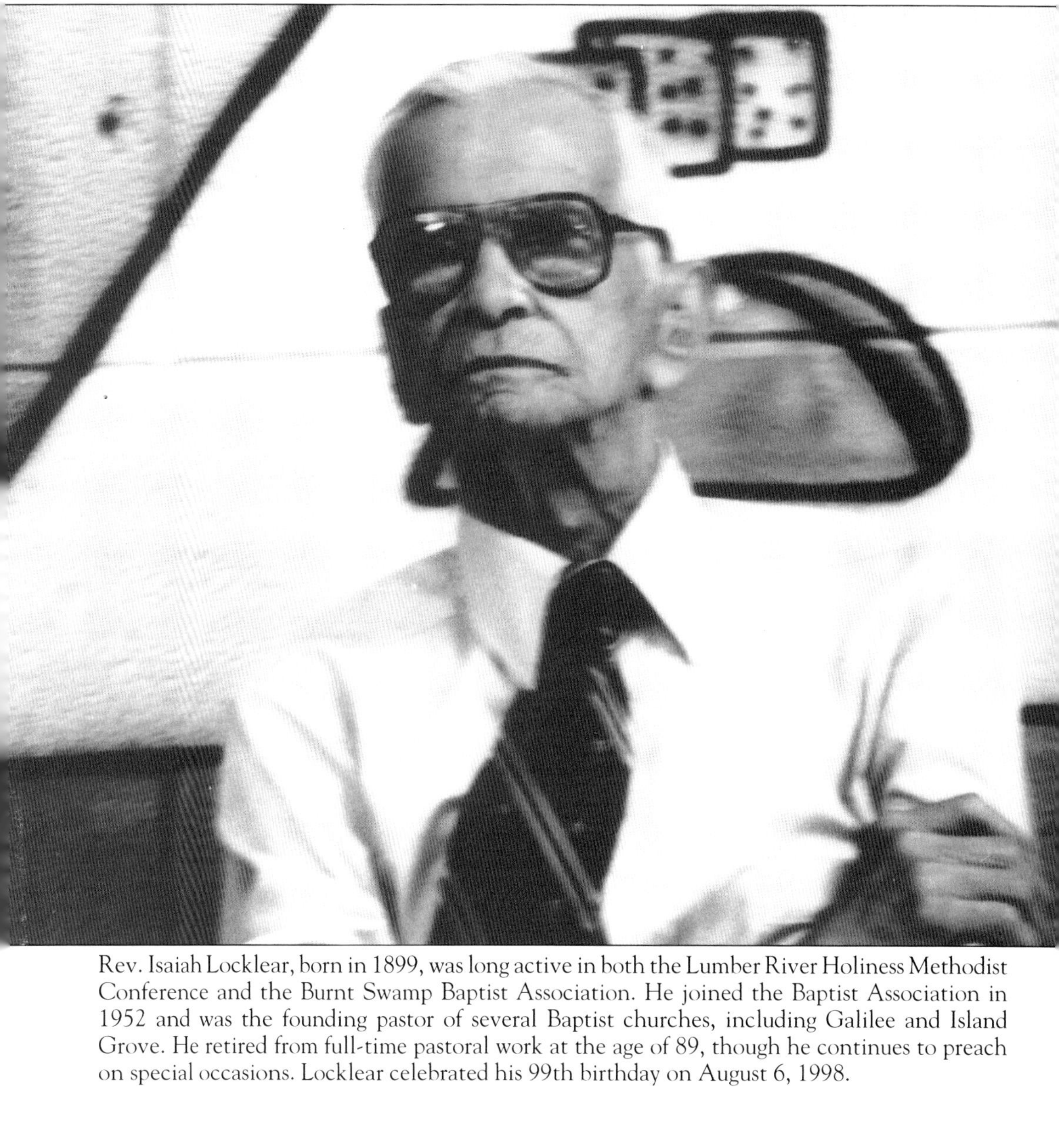

Rev. Isaiah Locklear, born in 1899, was long active in both the Lumber River Holiness Methodist Conference and the Burnt Swamp Baptist Association. He joined the Baptist Association in 1952 and was the founding pastor of several Baptist churches, including Galilee and Island Grove. He retired from full-time pastoral work at the age of 89, though he continues to preach on special occasions. Locklear celebrated his 99th birthday on August 6, 1998.

Rev. Joseph Anderson was a beloved minister with the Lumber River Holiness Methodist Conference. He had a reputation as a great prayer warrior and served as the pastor of all the churches in the conference, with the exception of Hopewell. Reverend Anderson was serving as the pastor of Shoeheel Holiness Methodist Church at his death in 1988.

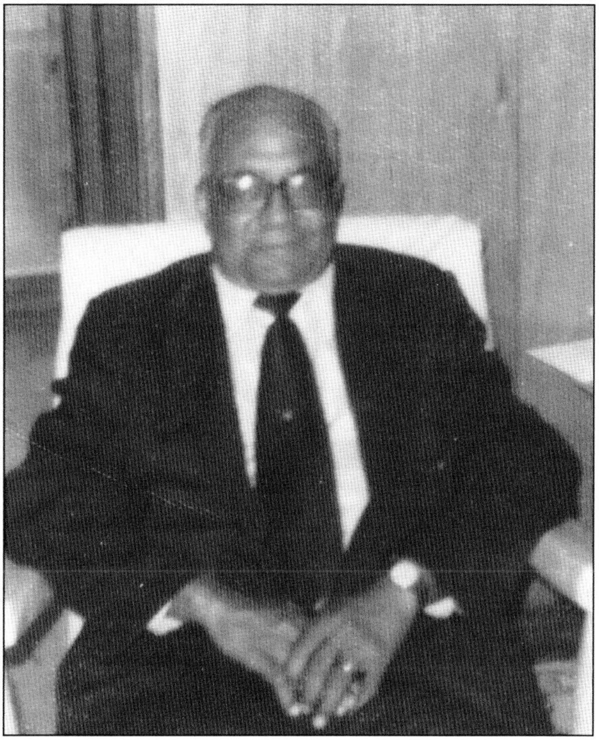

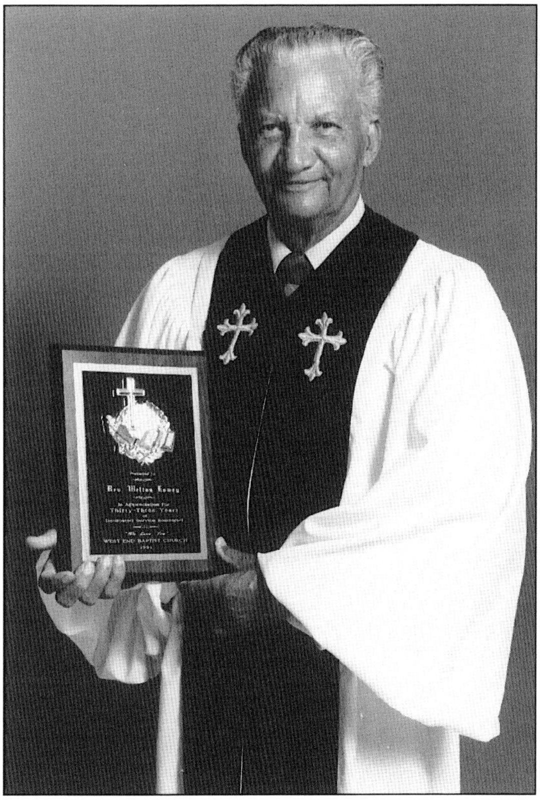

Rev. Wleton Lowry served as the pastor of West End Baptist Church in Lumberton for 33 years. Lowry graduated from what was the Indian Normal School in 1933 with a "B" teaching certificate, earned his bachelor of science degree at Pembroke State College in 1947, and his master's degree at George Peabody College in Nashville, Tennessee, in 1953. A local oral historian, Dr. Lowry is called on often to share Lumbee history. He was also a schoolteacher for 30 years.

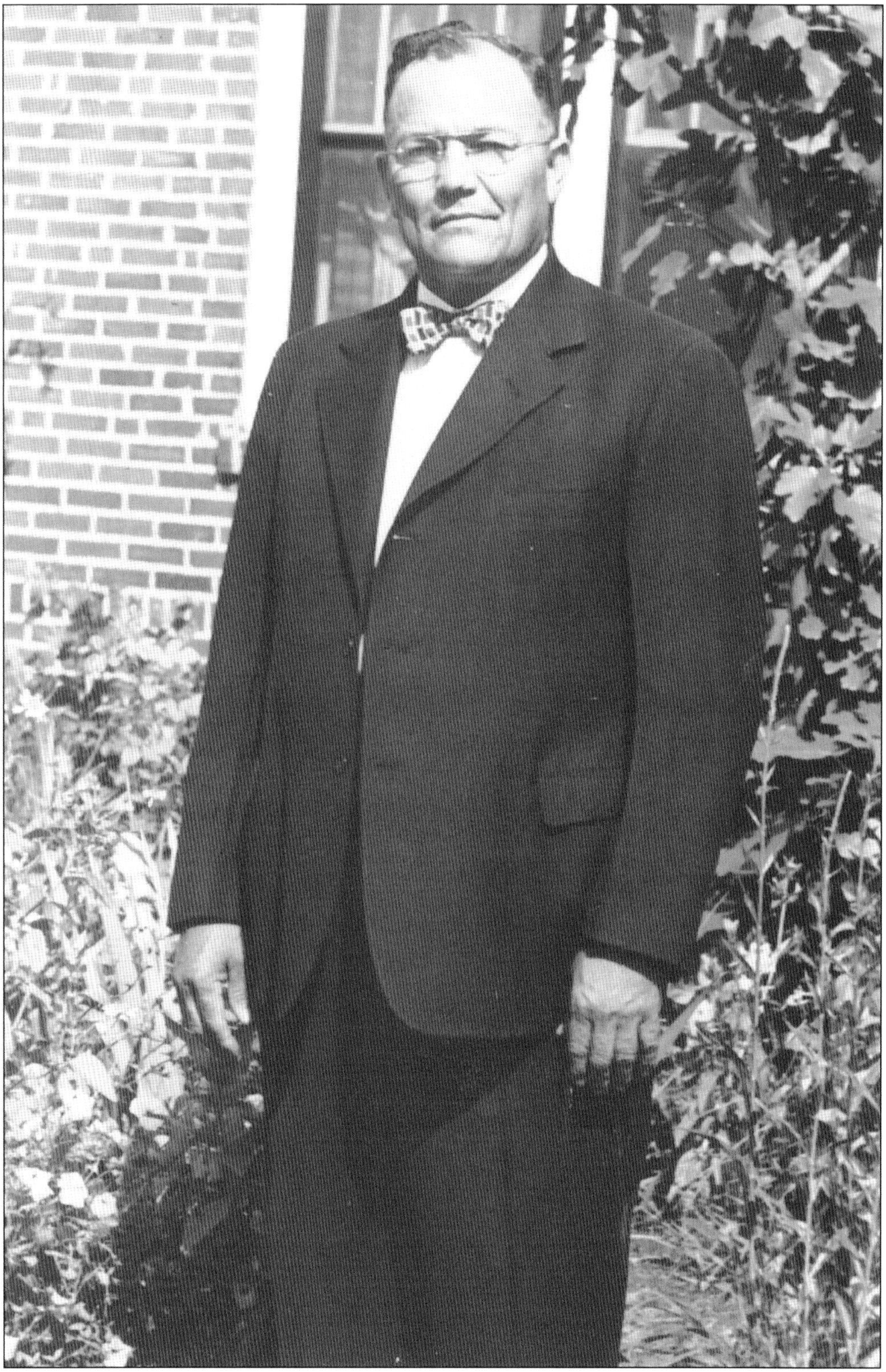

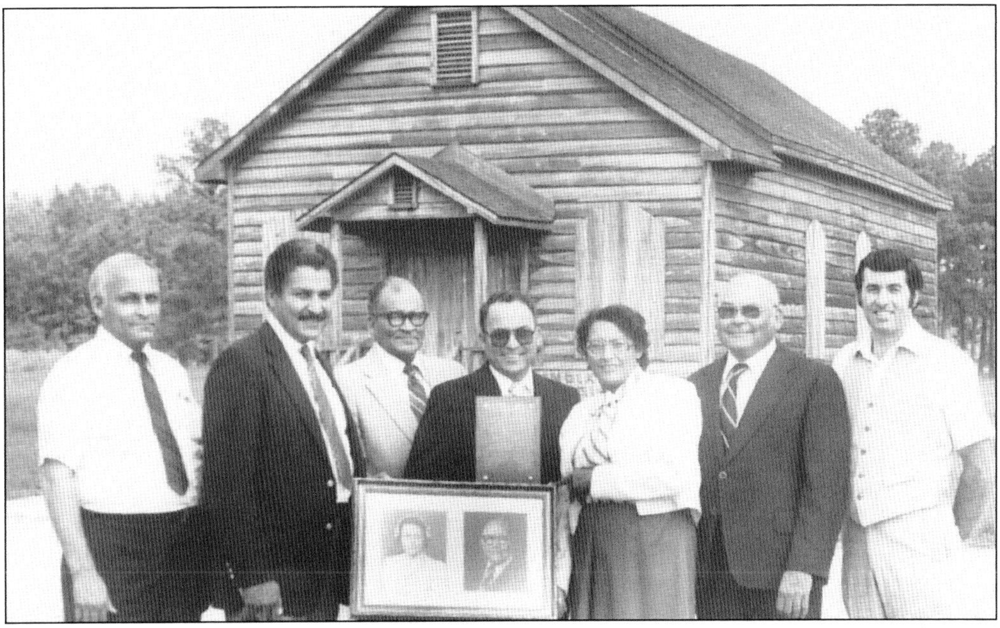

Shown here are the children of the late Reverend and Mrs. C.E. Locklear. They donated a portrait of Reverend and Mrs. Locklear to the museum, which was established by the Burnt Swamp Baptist Association. The building itself is that of the church that began the association and was named Burnt Swamp Baptist. Shown, from left to right, are Rev. Joel Garth Locklear, Roderick G. Locklear, the late William Castor Locklear, Bundy Ross Locklear, Vera Doris Locklear Malcolm, Clarence F. (Ted) Locklear, and Rev. Tony Brewington, who established the museum in his position as the director of missions for the Burnt Swamp Baptist Association. Reverend Brewington is now serving as the pastor of Mt. Elim Baptist Church in nearby Hoke County.

Opposite: Rev. C.E. Locklear was the first Native American elected as mayor of the town of Pembroke. He was elected in 1947 and served for four years, two consecutive two-year terms. Reverend Locklear was also a leading businessman and very active in the Burnt Swamp Baptist Association, where he served as the pastor of several local Baptist churches.

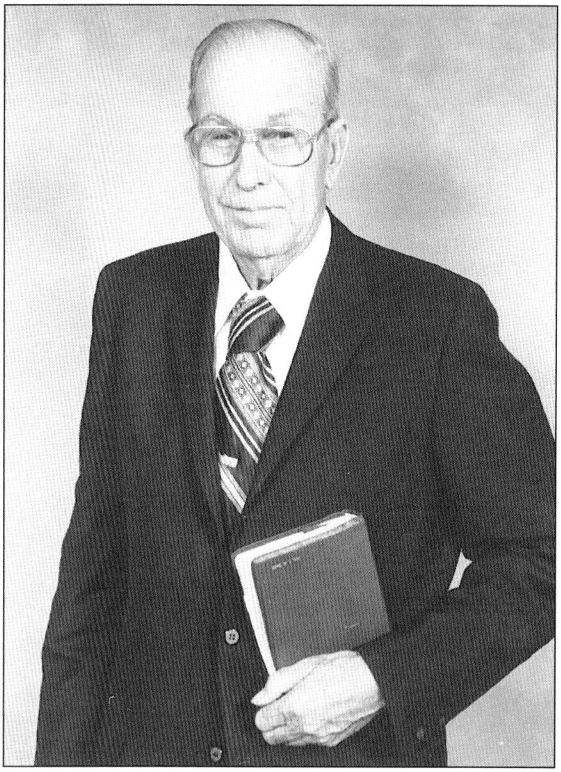

Rev. T.M. "Preacher Tommy" Swett served as the pastor of Bear Swamp Baptist Church approximately 40 years, beginning in 1943. He was well known for his preaching and his prayer life. Reverend Swett died in 1985.

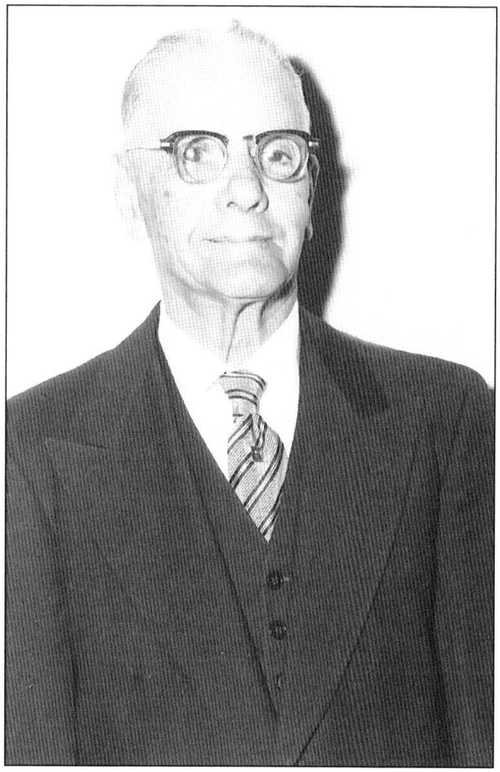

Rev. D.F. Lowry was an outstanding minister in the United Methodist Conference (UMC), in which he served in many capacities. He is shown preaching at Prospect United Methodist Church in 1946 when he served as pastor. Rev. Lowry led the effort to designate the Native Americans in the area as Lumbee in 1953.

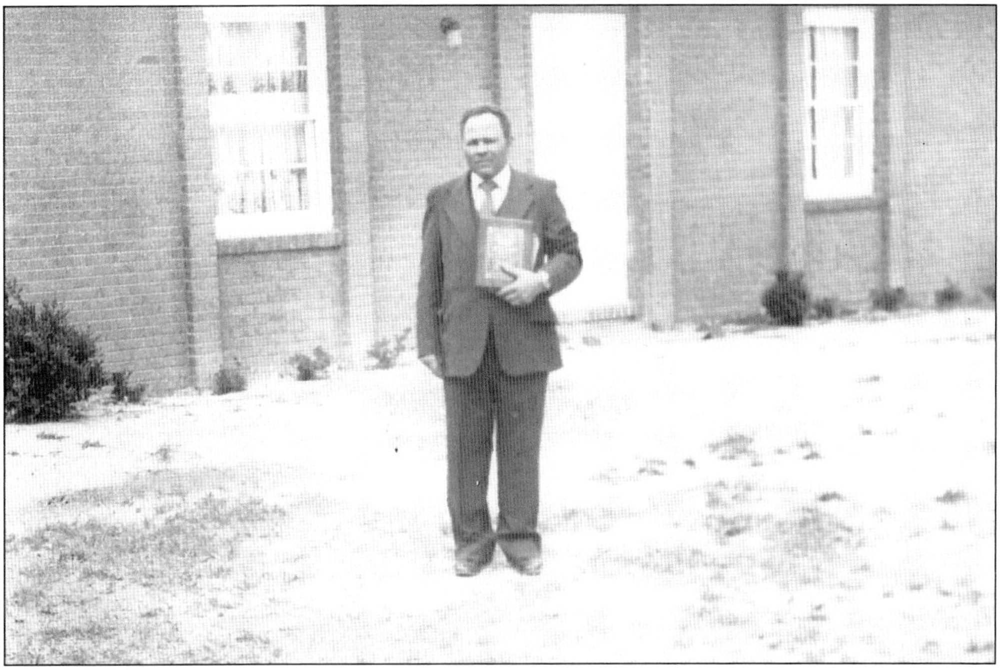

Rev. Manford Locklear served as the pastor of Beulah Baptist Church for 19 years, from 1972 until 1989. He now serves as the pastor of Mt. Moriah in Lumberton, North Carolina. Both churches are members of the Burnt Swamp Baptist Association.

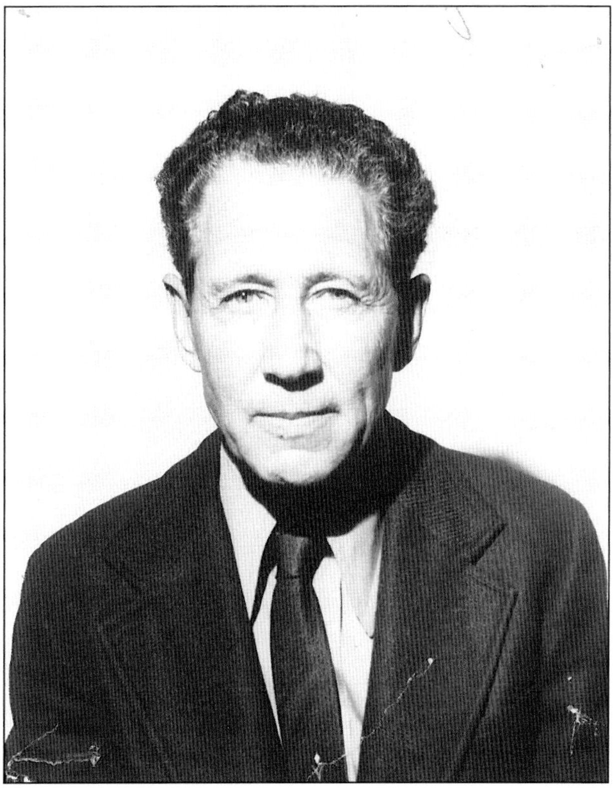

Rev. Joseph Lowry poses for a photograph. He is a Baptist minister who organized Lowry's Chapel in Hoke County.

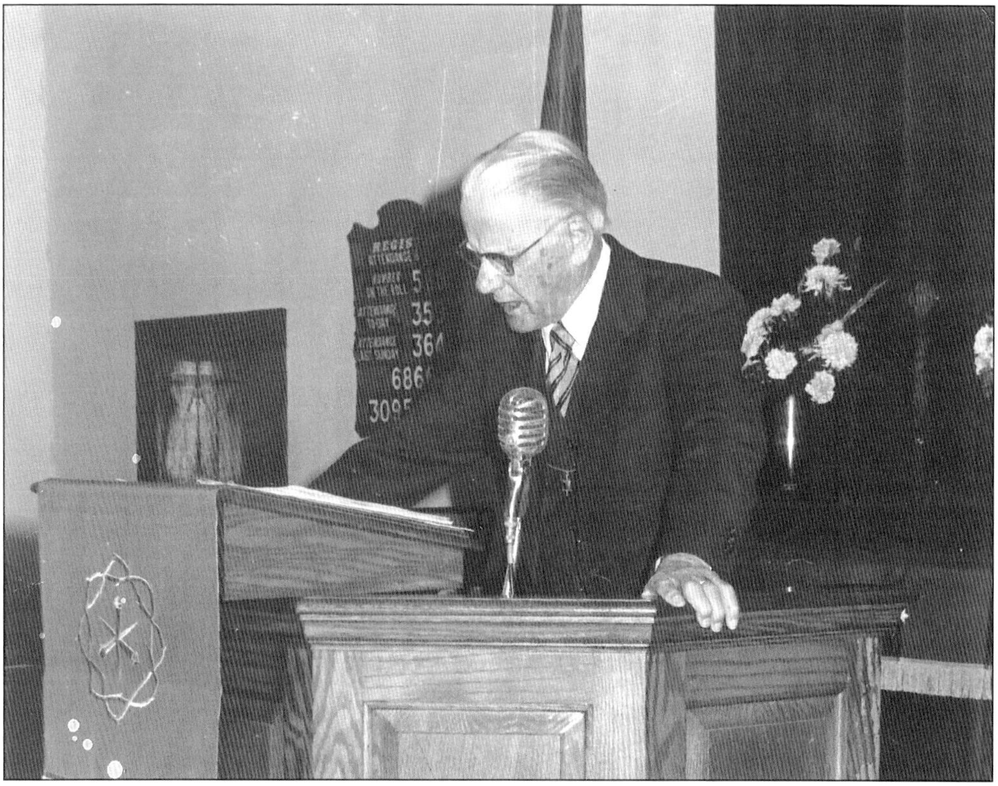

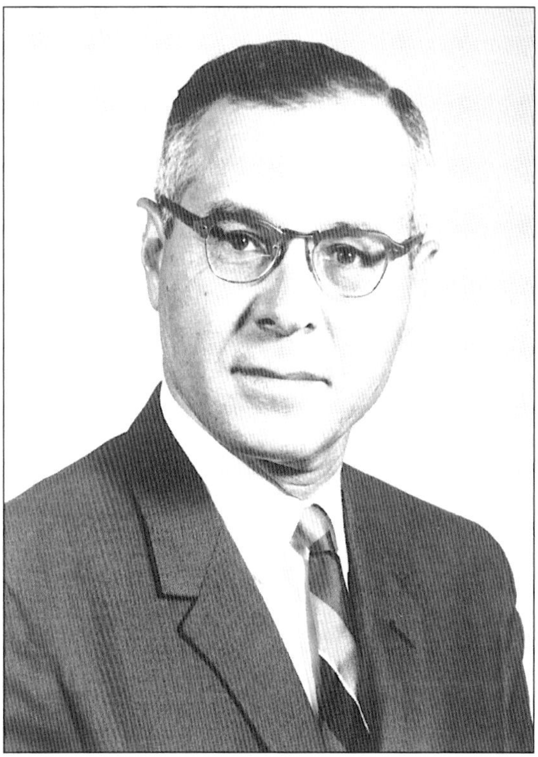

Rev. D.F. Lowry is shown in 1947 in the pulpit at Prospect United Methodist Church, where he served as pastor during the late 1940s. Lowry is a descendant of James Lowrie, a large landowner in Robeson County who flourished from 1758 to 1810. Rev. D.F. Lowry was educated in the county schools, and he was the first graduate of Croatan Normal School in 1905. He served for 20 years as a principal and educator in the county and was instrumental in the movement of the Normal School from Pates to the present site of the University of North Carolina at Pembroke.

Rev. Harvey L. Brewington served as the first Associational Missionary for the Burnt Swamp Baptist Association. He also served as the Baptist Student Union Director at Pembroke State College.

Dr. Dalton Peter Brooks is the pastor of Dundarrach Baptist Church, which he has served for 25 years, and is the moderator of the Burnt Swamp Baptist Association Union. He retired from Pembroke State University in 1996. Dr. Brooks was elected the first tribal chairman under the Lumbee Constitution of Cheraw Indians in 1994. He served for four years and chose not to seek re-election.

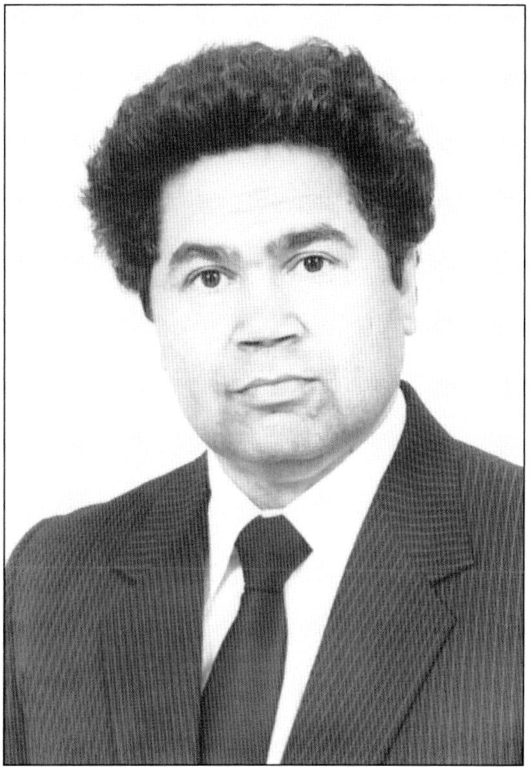

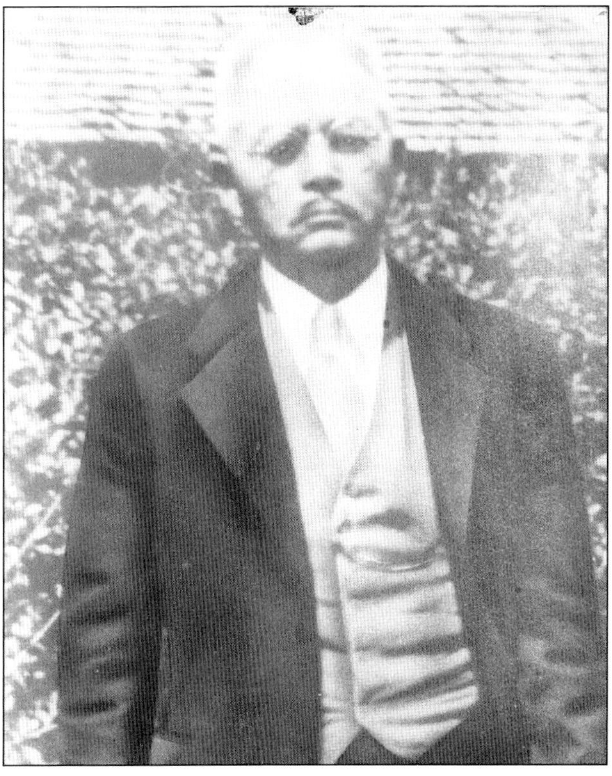

Rev. J. Ed Hunt was never known to pastor a church. In the early 1900s, he traveled from house to house and held house services where he preached to neighbors who gathered for that occasion. Many elders remember Ed Hunt holding services at their homes when they were children.

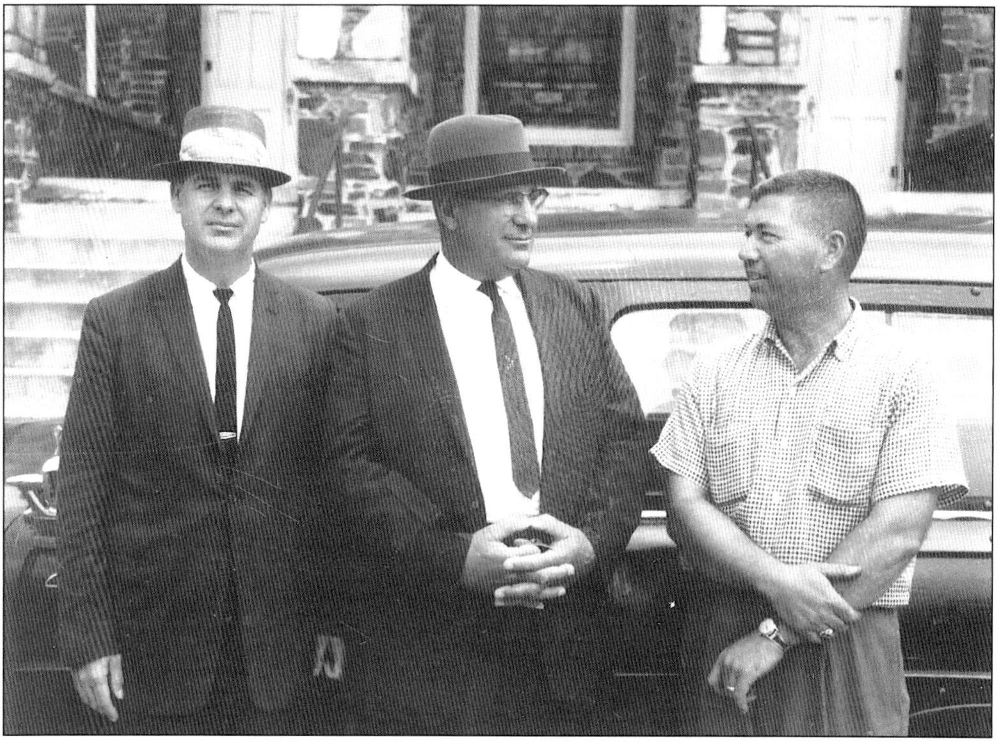

Southern Baptists presented a stationwagon to Rev. Dawley Maynor (center) of Pembroke in 1957.

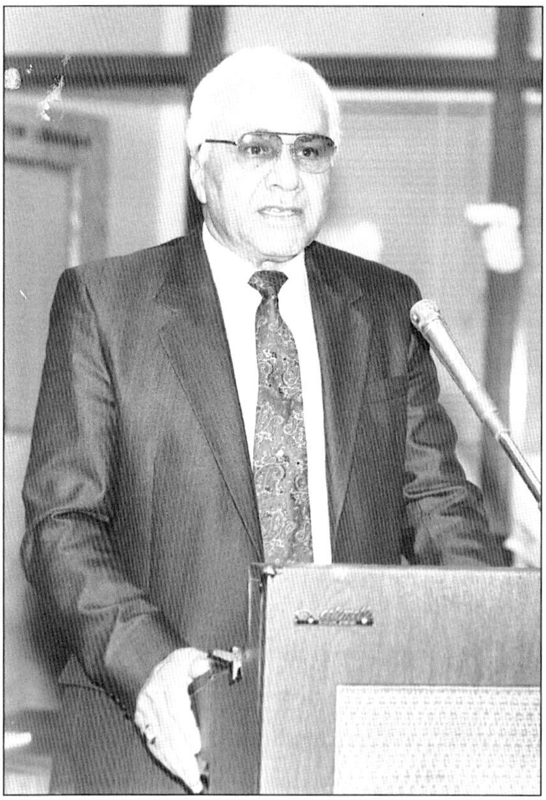

Rev. Julian Ransom served as the pastor of Cherokee Chapel United Methodist Church in Wakulla, North Carolina. Reverend Ransom retired as purchasing agent at PSU on December 31, 1983. He has served as the pastor of Cherokee Chapel Holiness Methodist Church since 1974. He gained additional fame for his portrayal of "the leader" in the outdoor drama *Strike at the Wind.*

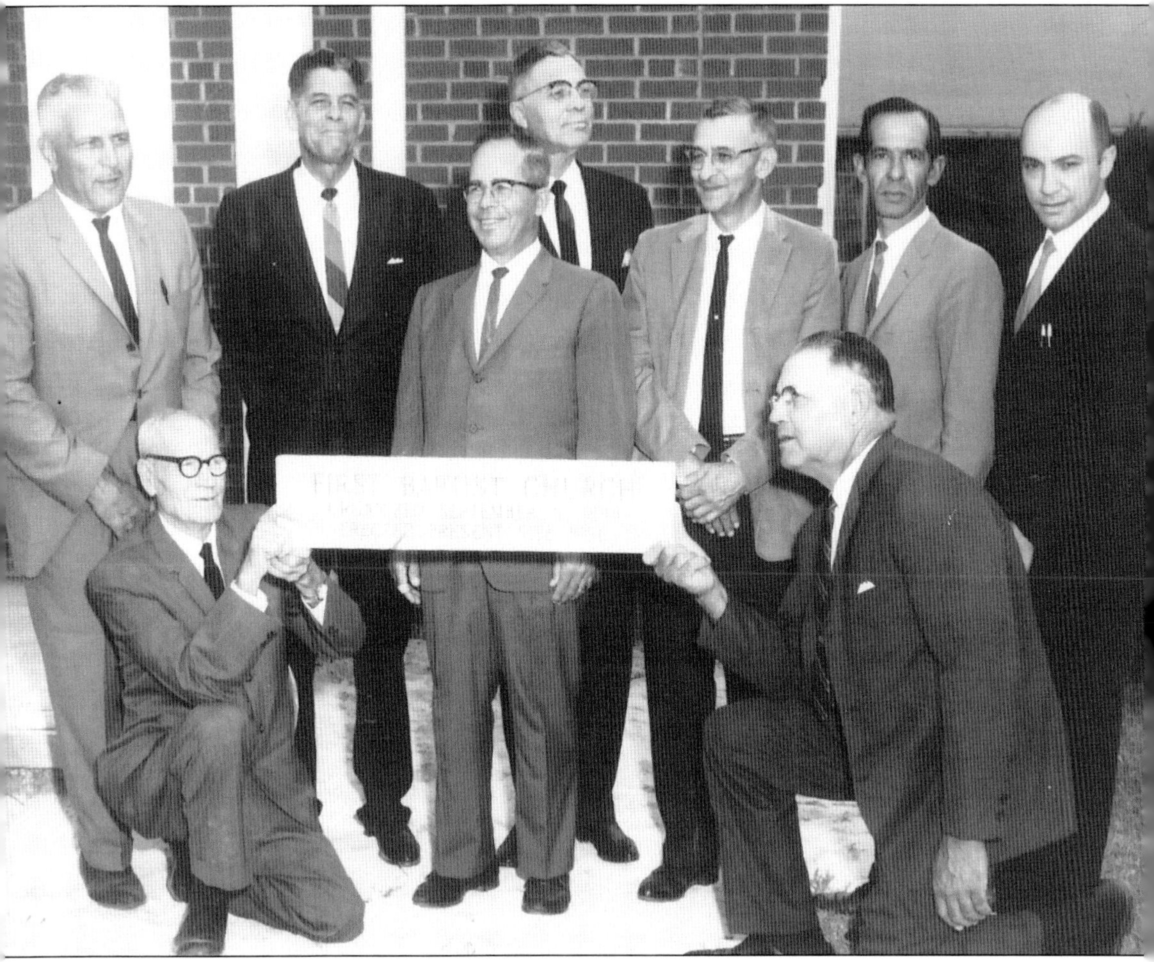

The First Baptist Church of Pembroke was organized on September 11, 1895. The present building on Union Chapel Road was erected in 1956. Shown here are some of the members of that congregation in 1956.

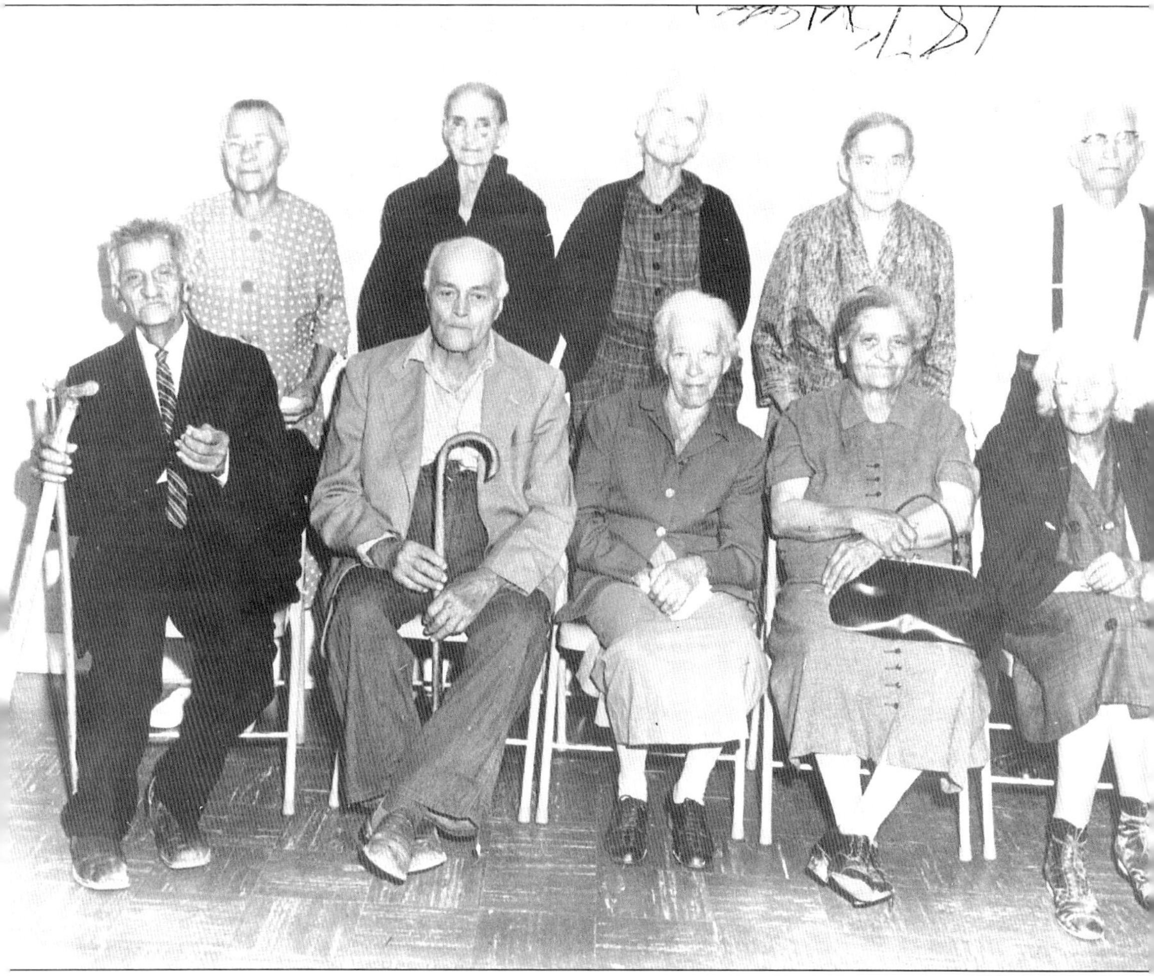

The Senior Adult Class of Prospect United Methodist Church is shown here in the early 1950s. From left to right are as follows: (seated) Rand Bullard, McClellan Locklear, Rency Barton, Eunice Bullard Locklear, and Mary Ellen Brayboy; (standing) Magnolia Locklear, Charlotte Jacobs, Emma J. Moore Bullard, Marie Sampson Moore, and Oakwind Brooks. Rand Bullard was the teacher.

Rev. S.A. Hammonds served in several capacities in the Saddletree community. Born June 30, 1874, he was the son of George Washington and Carolina Hammonds. He and his wife, Margaret Bell Hammonds, were the parents of seven children—Doshie, Stevie, Henry, Dennis, Mary, Lela, and Eunice. Reverend Hammond attended Pembroke Normal School in 1894 and Pembroke State College from 1906 until 1912. He was the moderator for the Burnt Swamp Association from 1930 until 1943. Among the Baptist churches he pastored were Reedy Branch, Mt. Airy, Mt. Moriah, Piney Grove, Ten Mile Center, Harper's Ferry, Berea, Bear Swamp, and Bethel Hill. He also taught in the public schools of Robeson County, and was very politically active. He was a member and leader for many years of the Red Man's Lodge in his community. Reverend Hammonds's daughter, Mrs. Lela Brooks, now 93, resides in Pembroke, as does his grandson, the Honorable Dexter Brooks, Senior Resident Superior Court Judge for Robeson County. Reverend Hammond died on April 6, 1951.

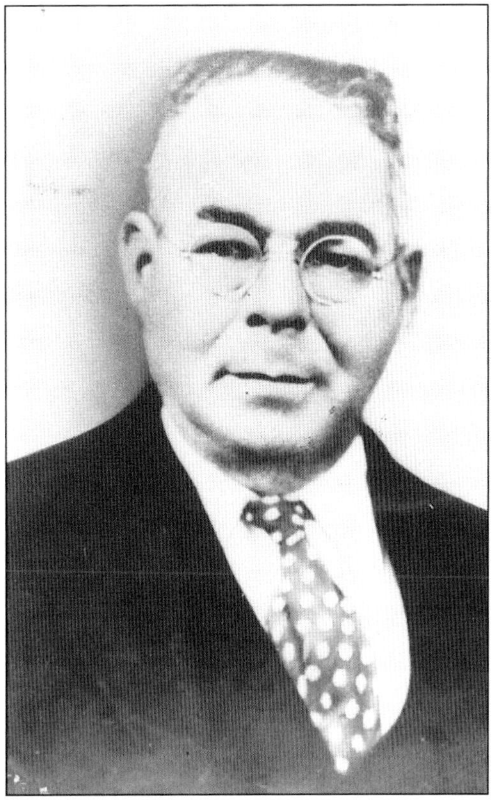

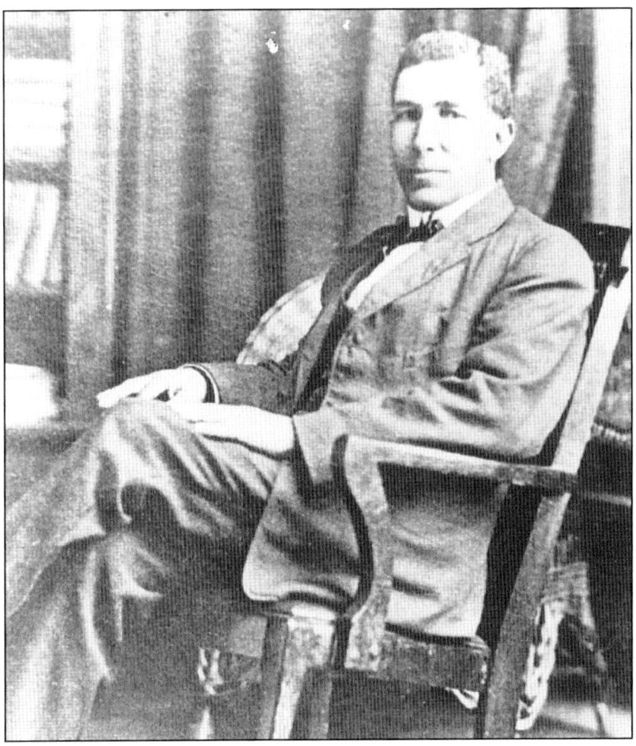

Rev. J.J. Bell was a grandson of Hardy Bell, one of the largest land owners in the Saddletree community. In 1859, the records listed Hardy Bell as the third largest landowner with 1,997 taxable acres in the county. Rev. J.J. Bell was a notable member of the Burnt Swamp Association and was politically active, serving as a member of the school committee for the Saddletree School District. He was appointed to this position in 1892, 1911, and 1916. Members of the school committee were the most politically powerful men in the Native American community. Reverend Bell also served as the moderator of the Burnt Swamp Association from 1910 to 1922.

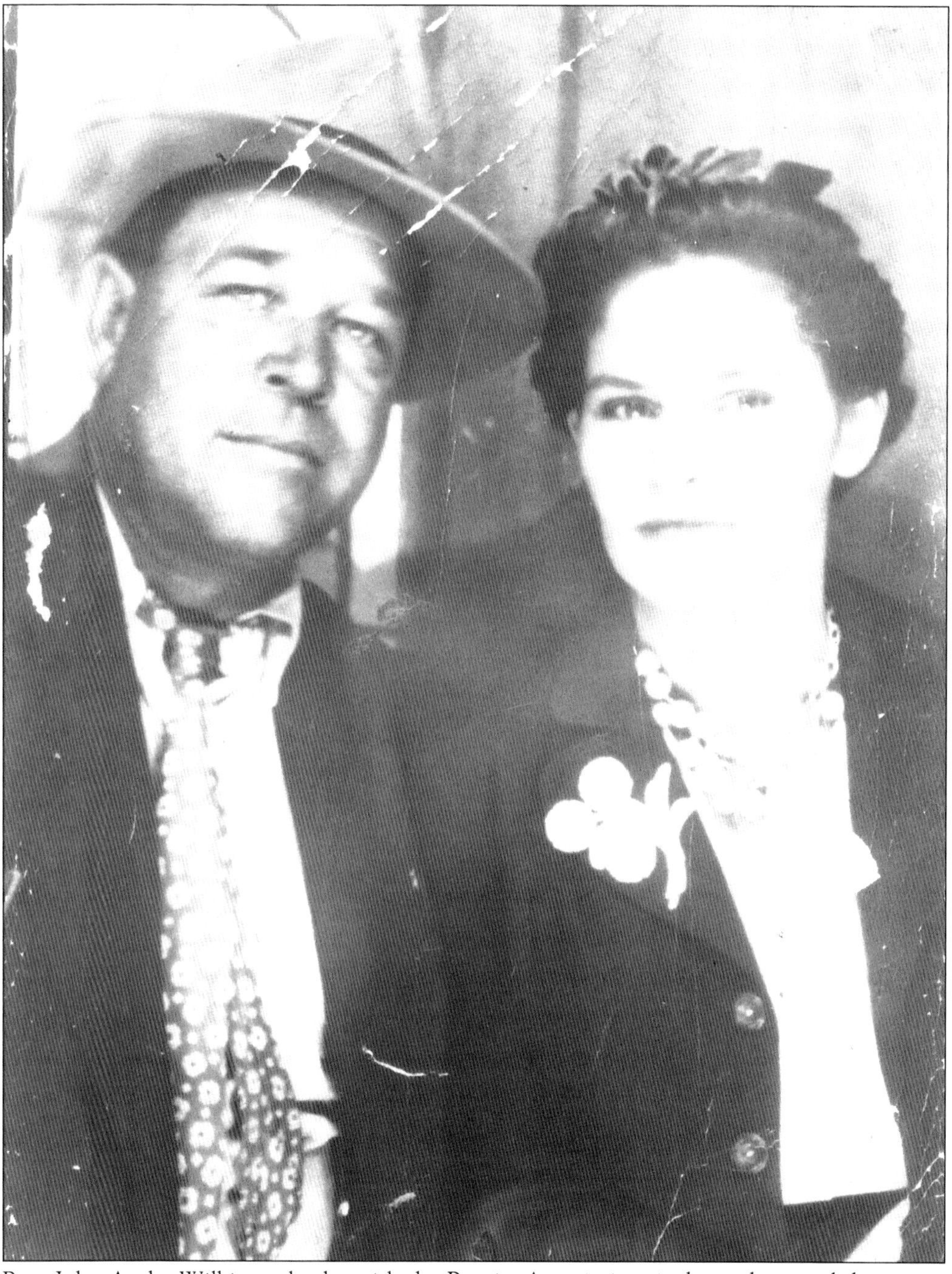

Rev. John Ander Wilkins, a leader with the Baptist Association, is shown here with his sister-in-law, Wessie Anderson Maynor, wife of the late Reverend Charlie Maynor.

Rev. C.S. Warriax was a spiritual leader from the Saddletree community. His son, Shelton Warriax, would gain national attention in 1958 as one of the individuals who routed the Ku Klux Klan in nearby Maxton, North Carolina.

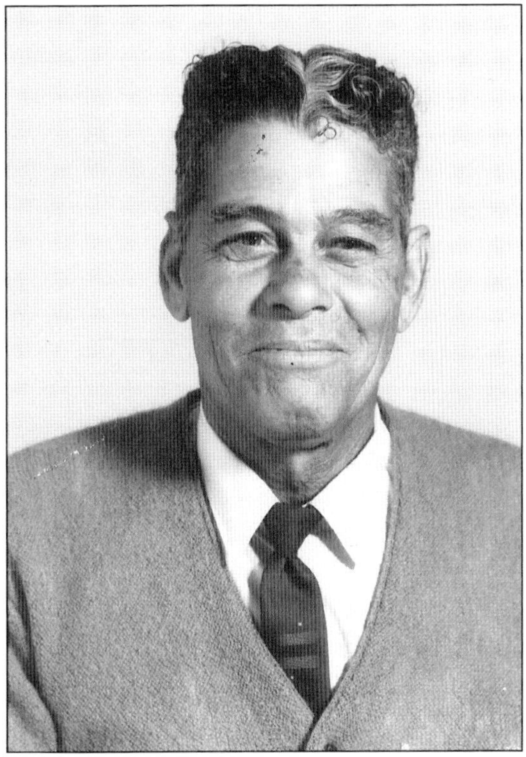

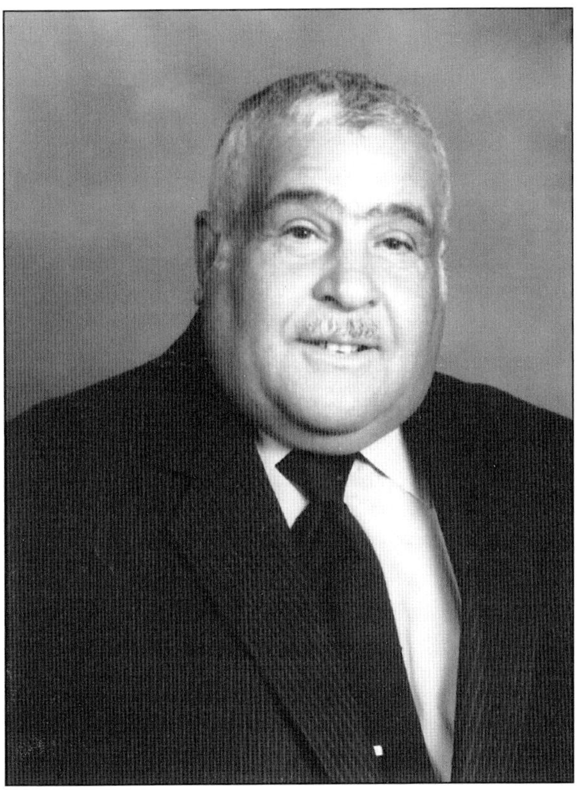

Rev. Ward Clark, a businessman and minister, served the Lumbee River Holiness Methodist Conference as bishop from 1974 to 1984. He was born on March 3, 1928, and died June 6, 1997. Reverend Clark also served for a short period as the president of the Lumbee River Electric Membership Corporation.

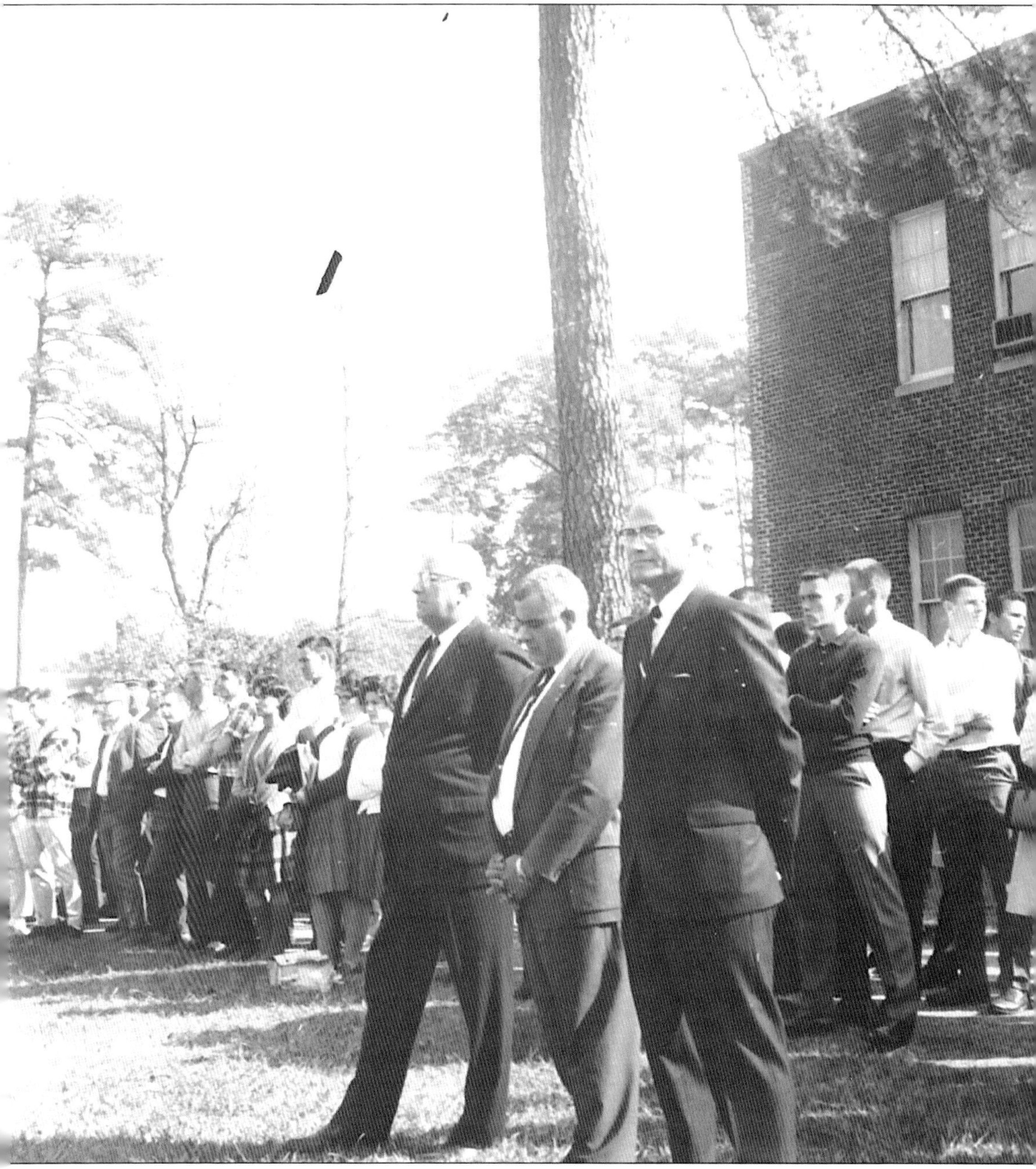

Shown here are Rev. Dawley Maynor (left), Sam Dial, and Rev. Venus Brooks at the Pembroke State College during a Veterans' Day ceremony in 1957.

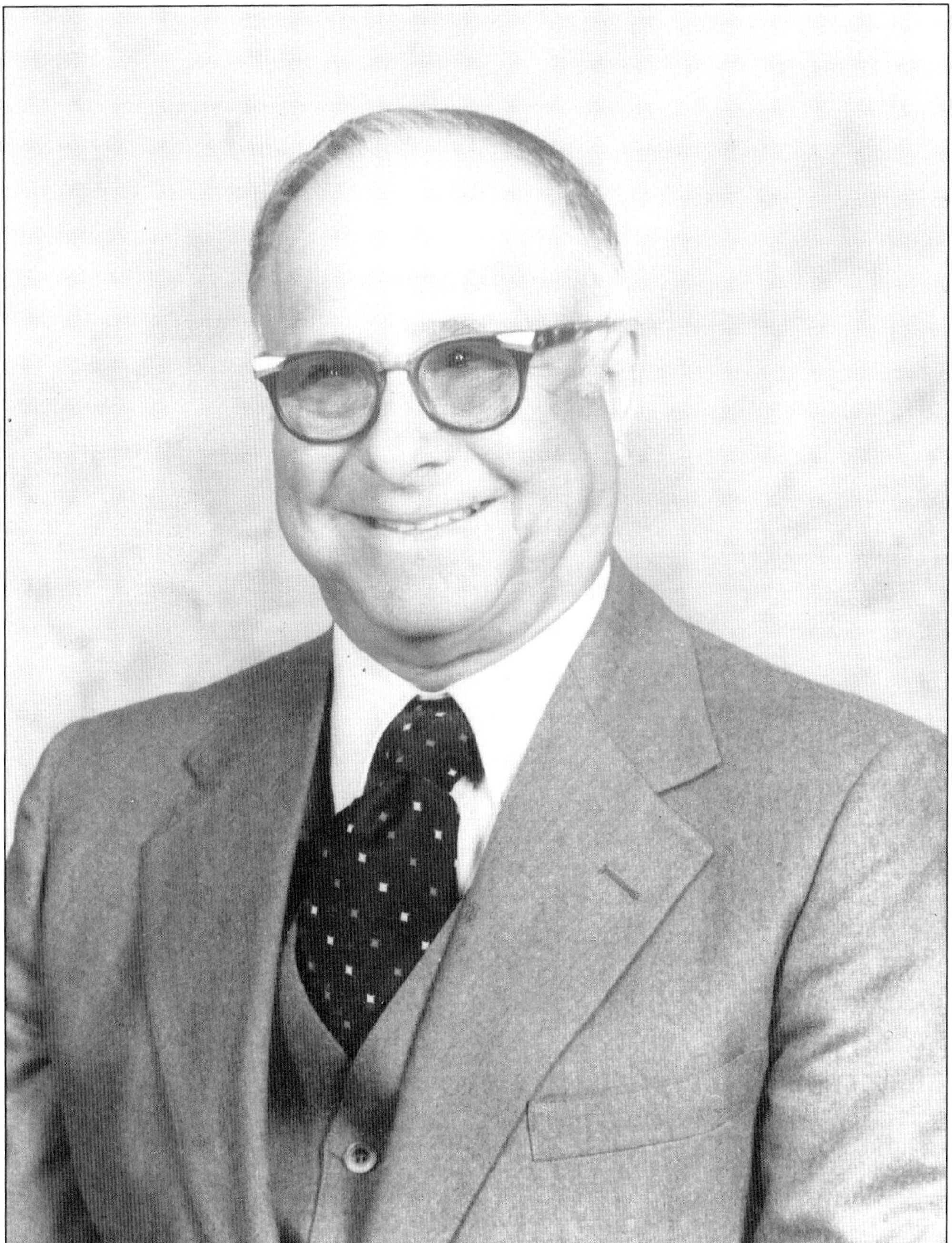

Rev. Willard Oxendine was active in the Lumber River Holiness Methodist Conference. One of the churches he pastored was New Prospect Holiness Methodist Church.

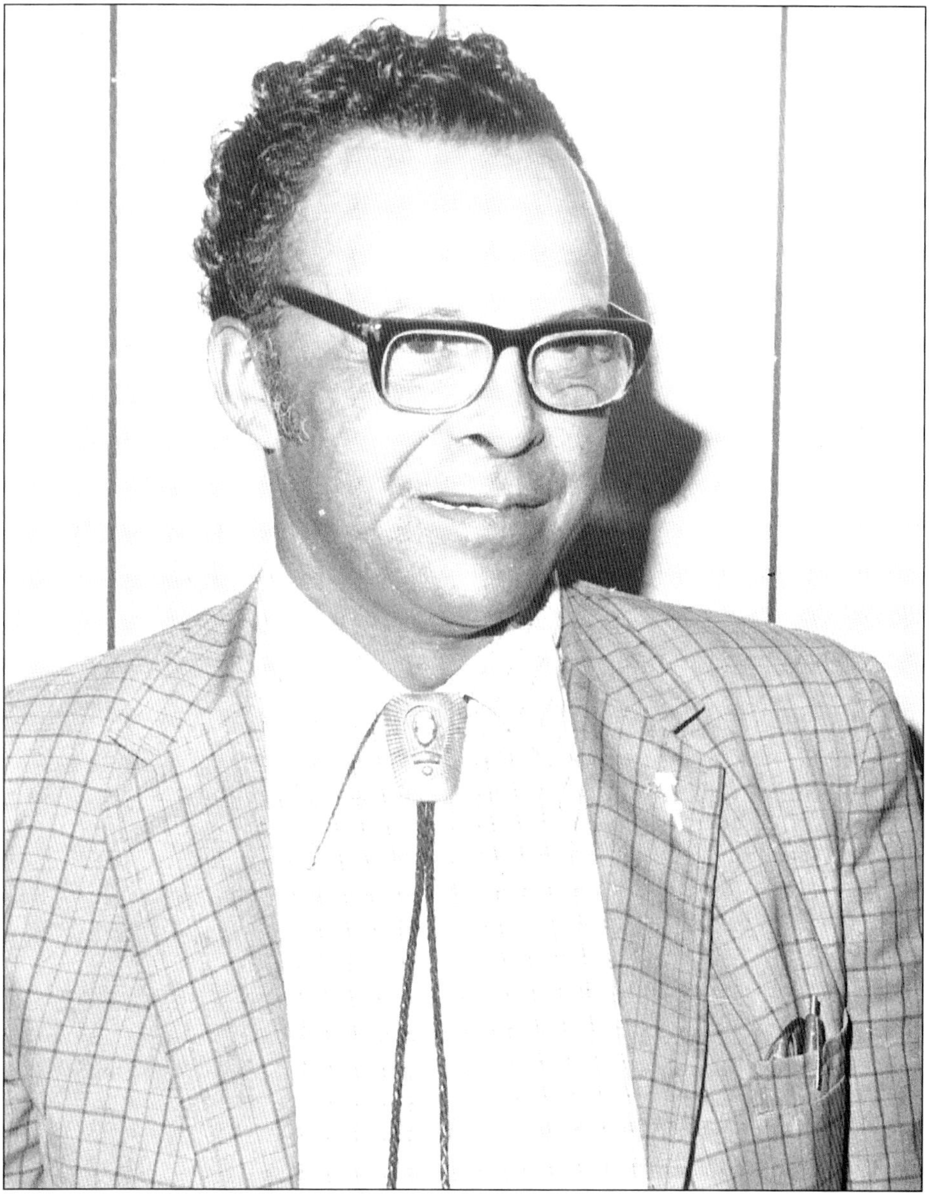

Rev. Elias Rogers was the first minority to serve on the Lumbee River Electric Membership Corporation, Red Springs, North Carolina. He was elected to that position in 1967 and subsequently was seated by a federal judge when the local whites, who had control of the local cooperative, refused to acknowledge his election. He endured many hardships as the only Native American on the board. In 1967, there was only one Native American employed at the multimillion-dollar cooperative. In the 20 years that followed, African Americans, as well as Native Americans, were elected to the board. The board is now made up entirely of Native Americans, the general manager is Native American, and Native Americans share equitable employment. Reverend Rogers was defeated for his seat in 1989 but remained active in the annual elections. He is recognized for his determination and audacity. His life story is recounted in a book he published in 1996 entitled *A Life of Discrimination*. Reverend Rogers died in 1998 at age 67. He resided in nearby Hoke County.

Three

Businesses and Local Government

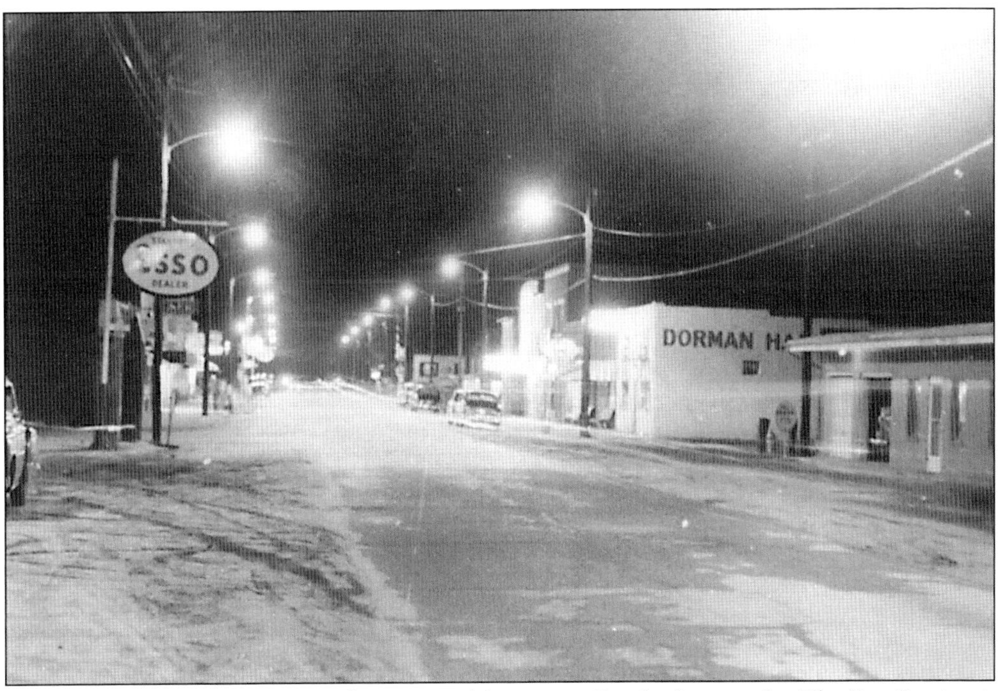

This photo was taken in 1959 and is a view of downtown Pembroke at night. The Esso Station is shown on the left. Later, it became known as the Roadrunner Service Center and was operated for 30 years by the late Vardell Ransom. The Pembroke Fire Department is shown to the right. This building would later house the Pembroke Police Department, the Clerk's Office, and the Magistrate's Office, which are still located there today.

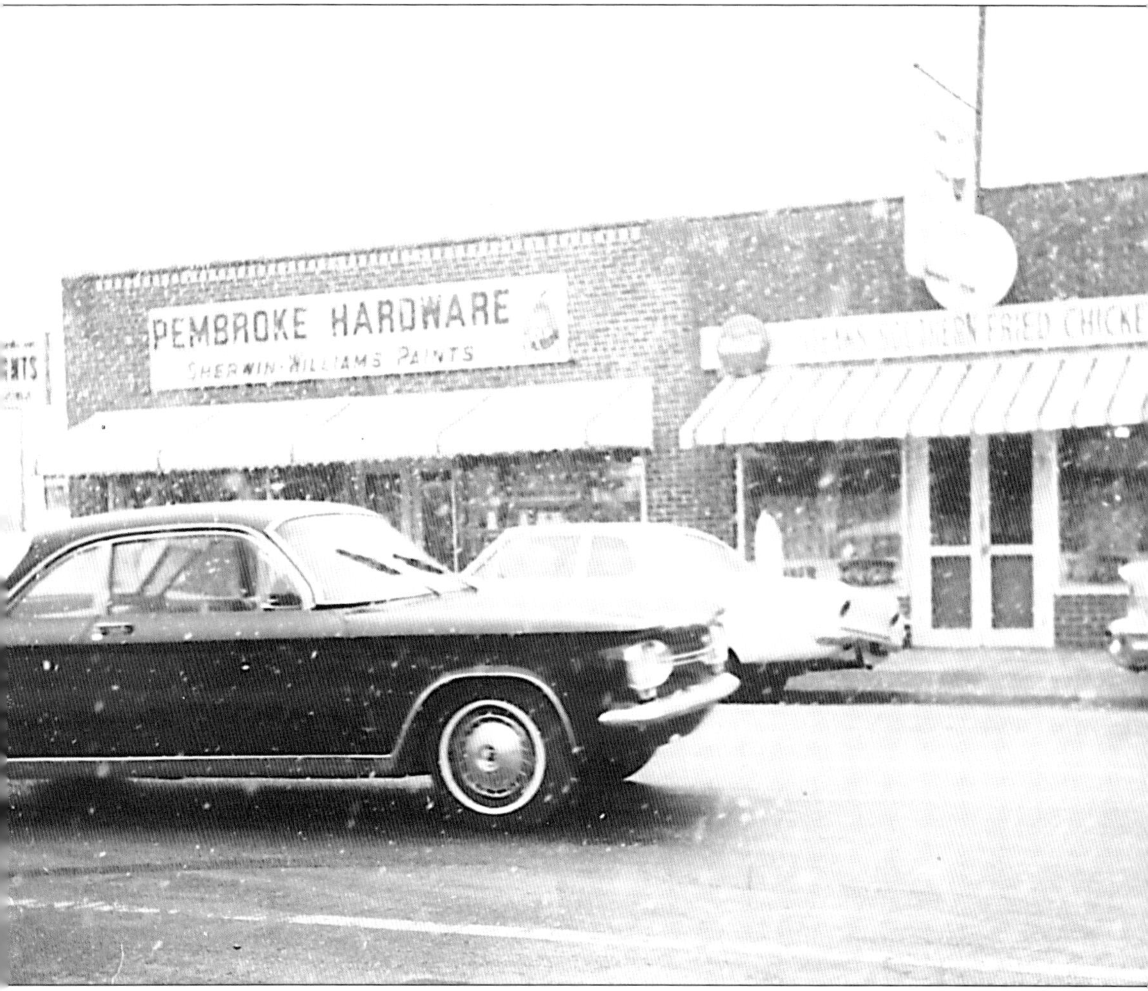

Pembroke Hardware is shown here before its renovation. In the 1960s, it was next door to Bell's Cafe. Later, Pembroke Hardware bought the adjoining property and then renovated and expanded their business until it covered almost the entire block.

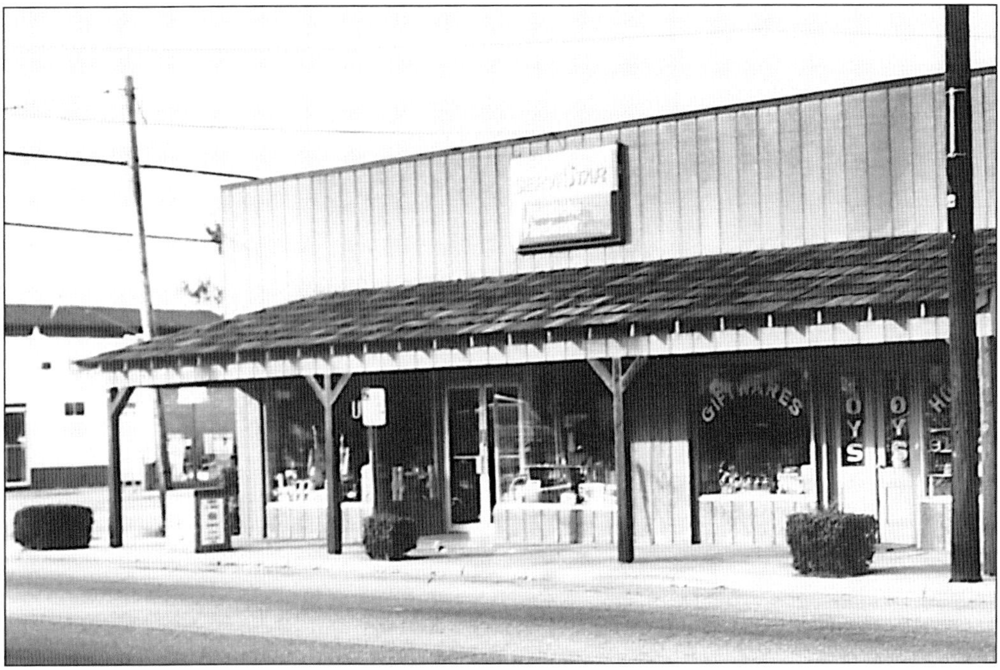

Pembroke Hardware, located on Main Street, was operated for many years by Mr. Curt Locklear. He has retired, and his sons, Lindsay and Steven Locklear, now operate the business. The building was renovated and expanded in 1989. Pembroke Hardware has been a part of the business community in Pembroke since the 1950s.

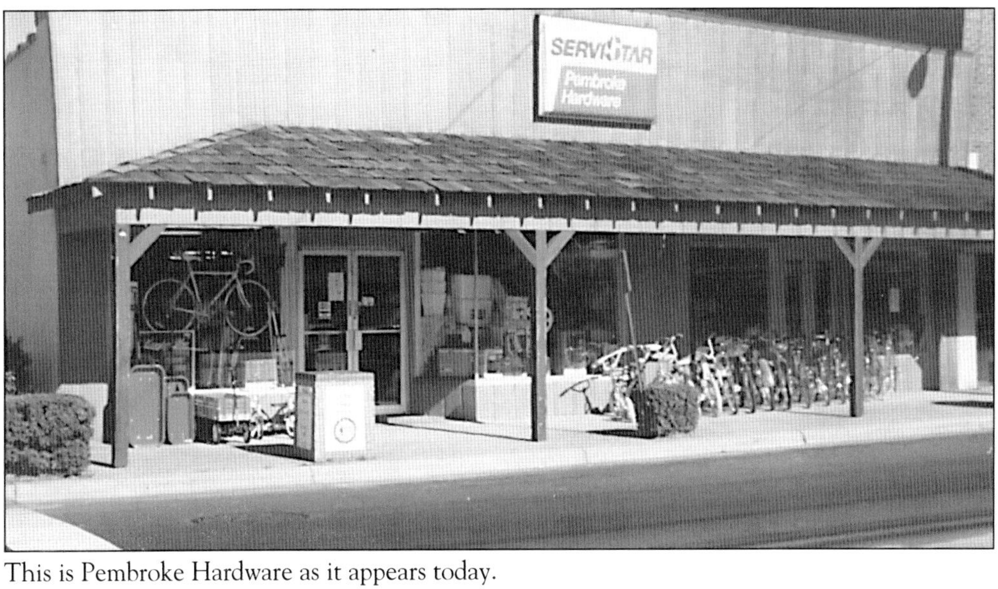

This is Pembroke Hardware as it appears today.

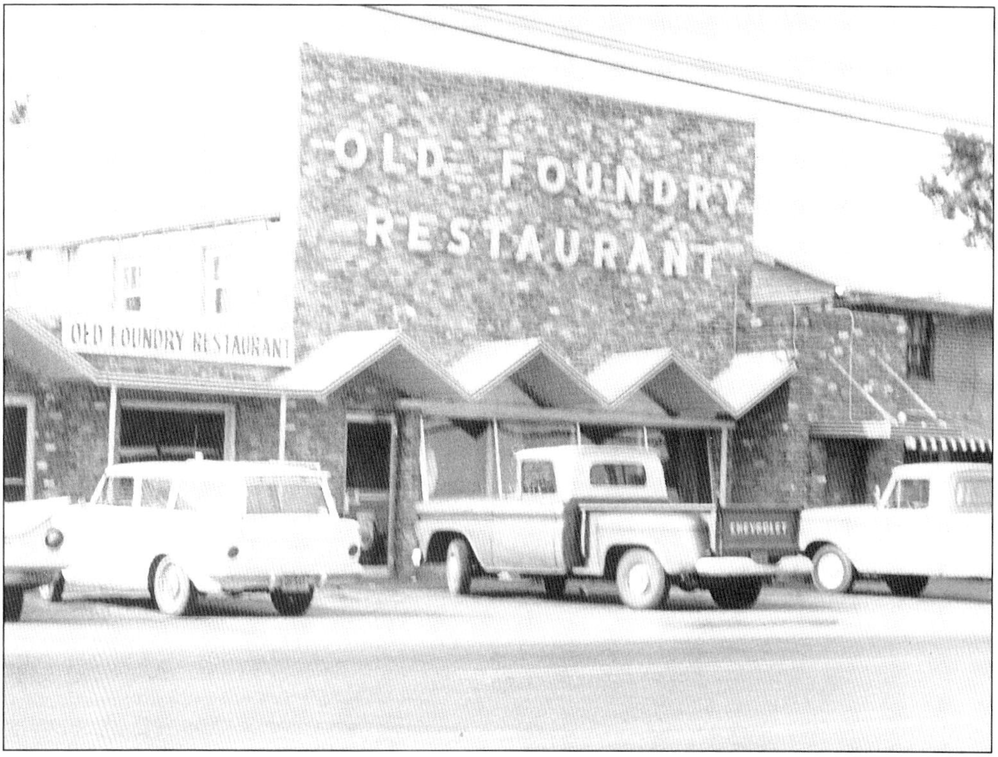

The Old Foundry Restaurant was the first Native American–owned restaurant in the city limits of Lumberton. This photograph was taken in 1966. The restaurant was owned and operated by the late Hilton Oxendine and his brother, Hubert Oxendine.

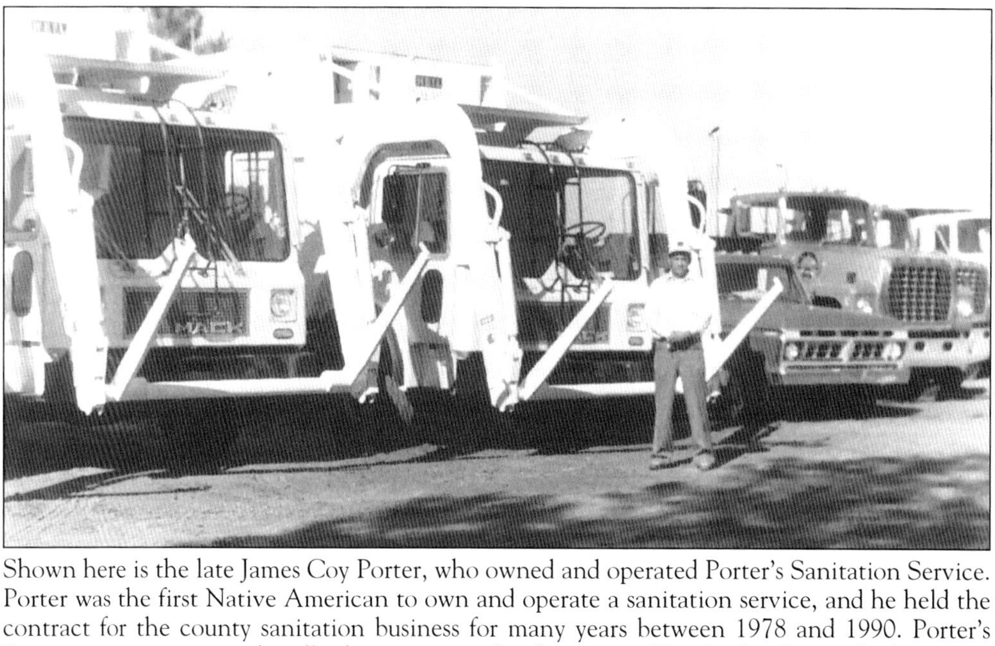

Shown here is the late James Coy Porter, who owned and operated Porter's Sanitation Service. Porter was the first Native American to own and operate a sanitation service, and he held the contract for the county sanitation business for many years between 1978 and 1990. Porter's Sanitation continues to handle the sanitation for the town of Pembroke. Porter died in 1996, and the business is still operated by his children.

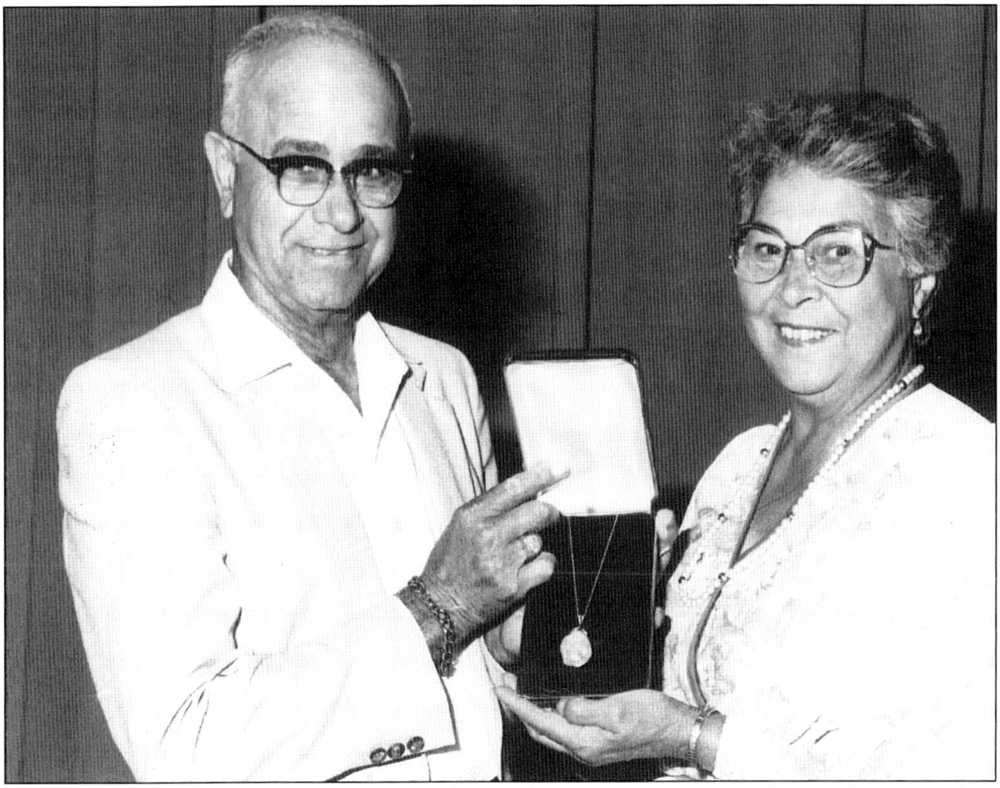

Hubert Oxendine, seen here with his wife, Mable Oxendine, operated Oxendine's Jewelers for many years. He was also active with the Pembroke Rescue Squad, one of the many civic activities in which he was involved.

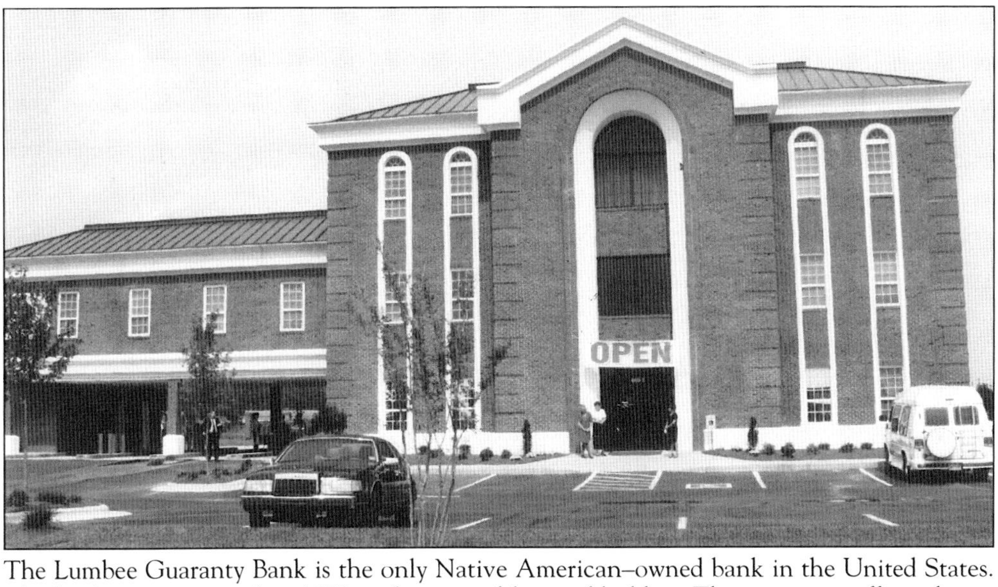

The Lumbee Guaranty Bank is the only Native American–owned bank in the United States. The bank was organized in 1972 and is owned by stockholders. The corporate offices shown above were built in 1998. Larry Chavis serves as the president, and Pembroke attorney Arnold Locklear is the chairman of the board of directors.

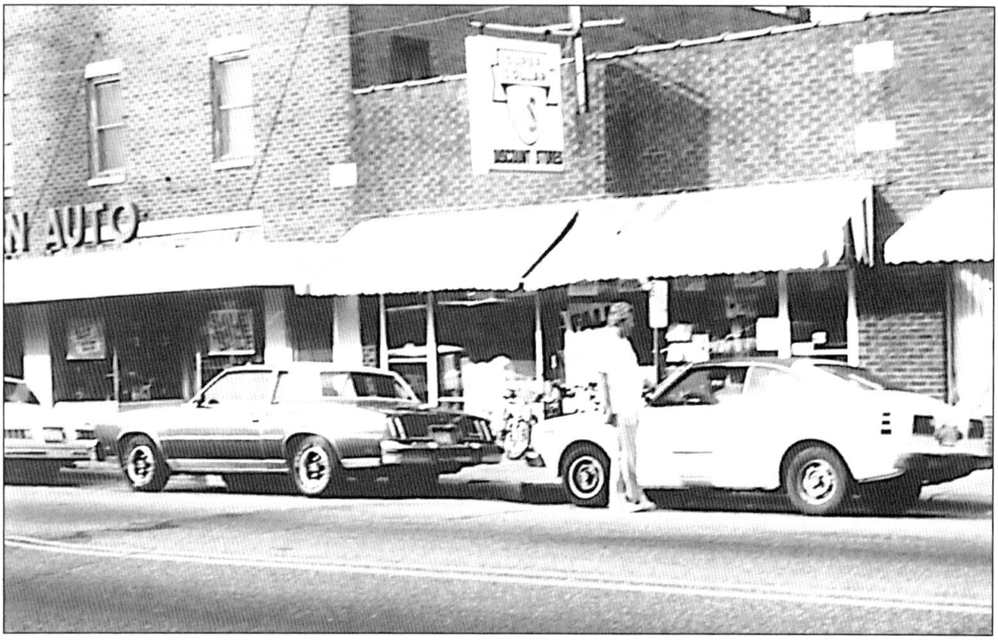

This is a view of the Super Dollar Store on West Third Street.

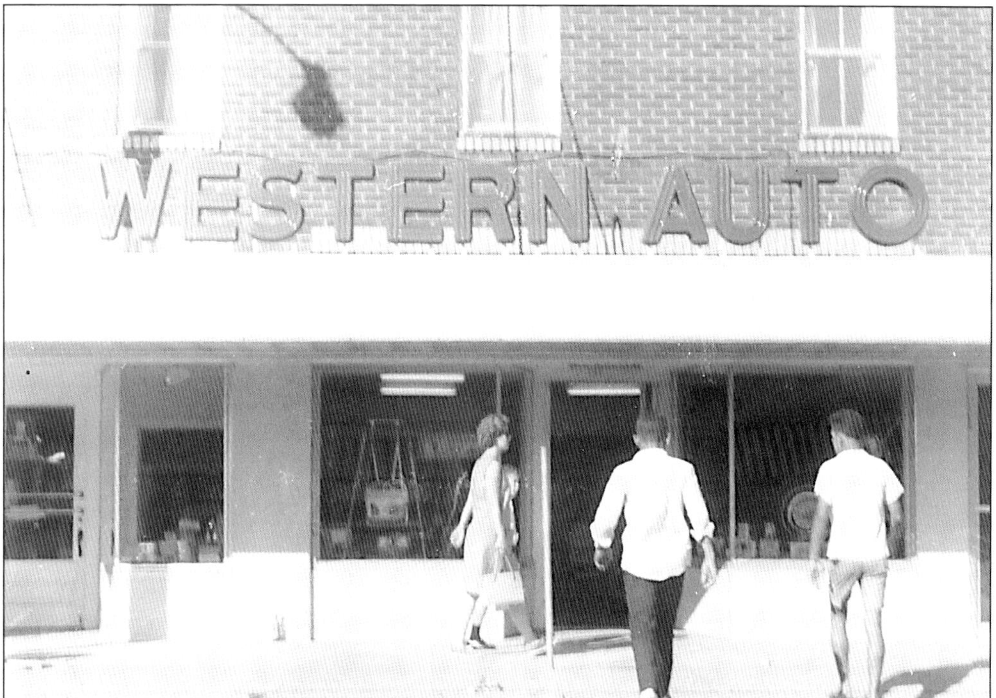

The Western Auto was located on West Third Street and was operated for many years by Lee Neville. The building, located down the street from Pembroke Hardware, later became part of the expansion of that business.

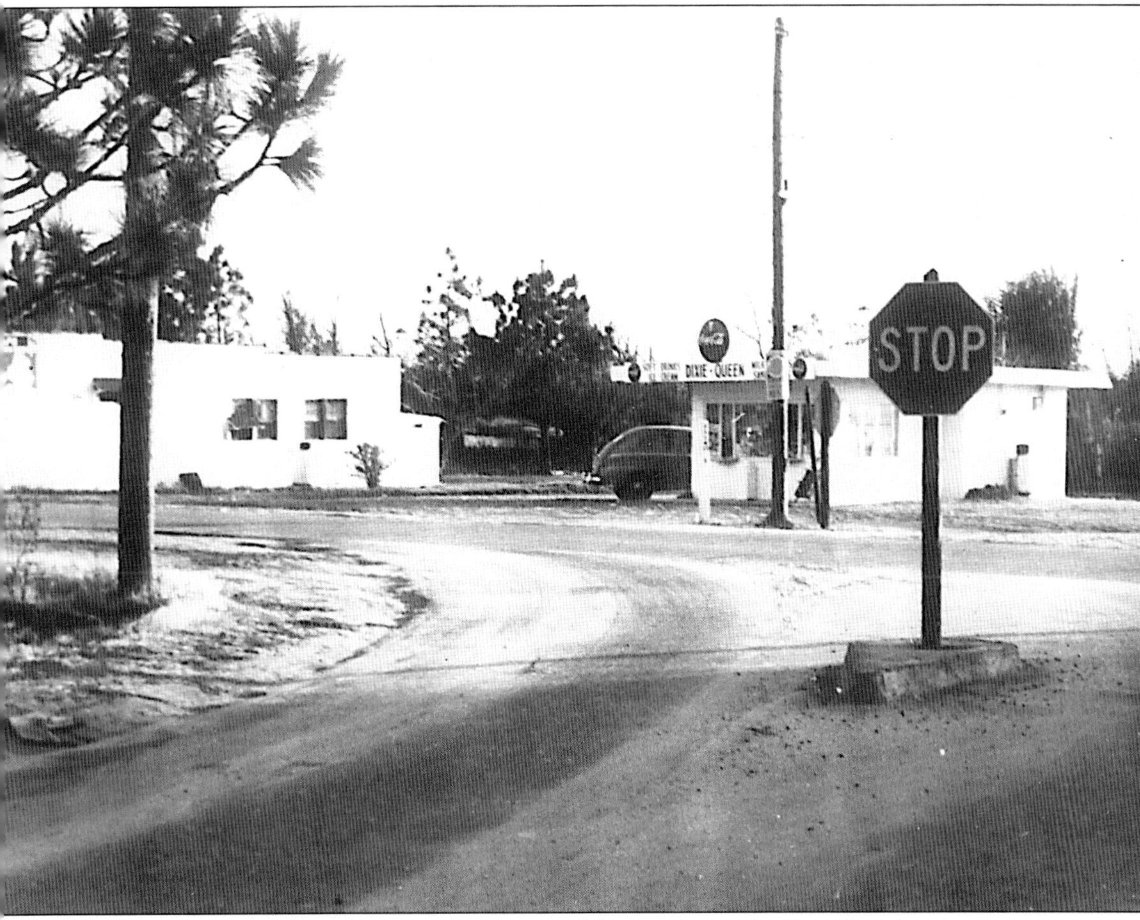

The Dixie Queen, seen here in 1955, was operated for many years by Dice Ann Sanderson.

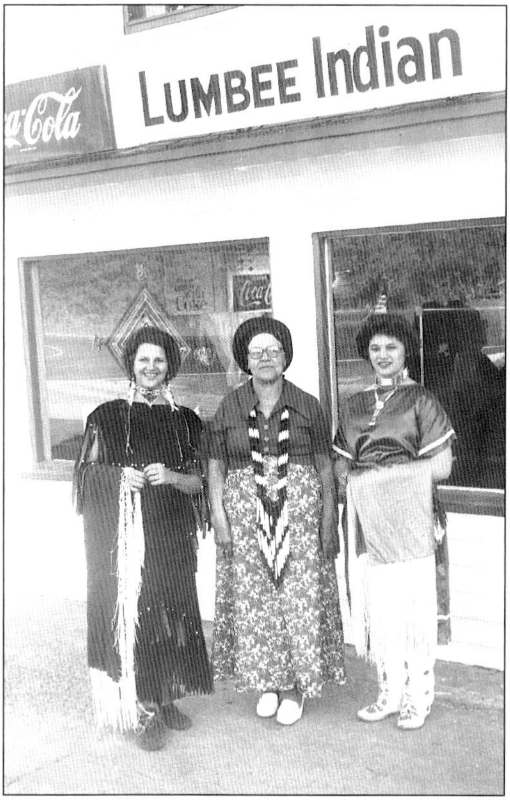

Mrs. Lucy Jane Chavis Oxendine (center), owner and operator of Lumbee Indian Arts and Crafts, poses here with her daughter Hope and an unidentified woman. Lucy operated the arts and crafts store out of the old Seaboard Grill building at the crossing of the railroad tracks on Union Chapel Road. She later moved the business to another location on U.S. Highway 74. Hope starred for many years in the outdoor drama *Strike at the Wind* as Rhoda, the wife of Henry Berry Lowrie.

This 1956 photograph shows the Log Cabin Service Station, which was operated for many years by Wesley Dial.

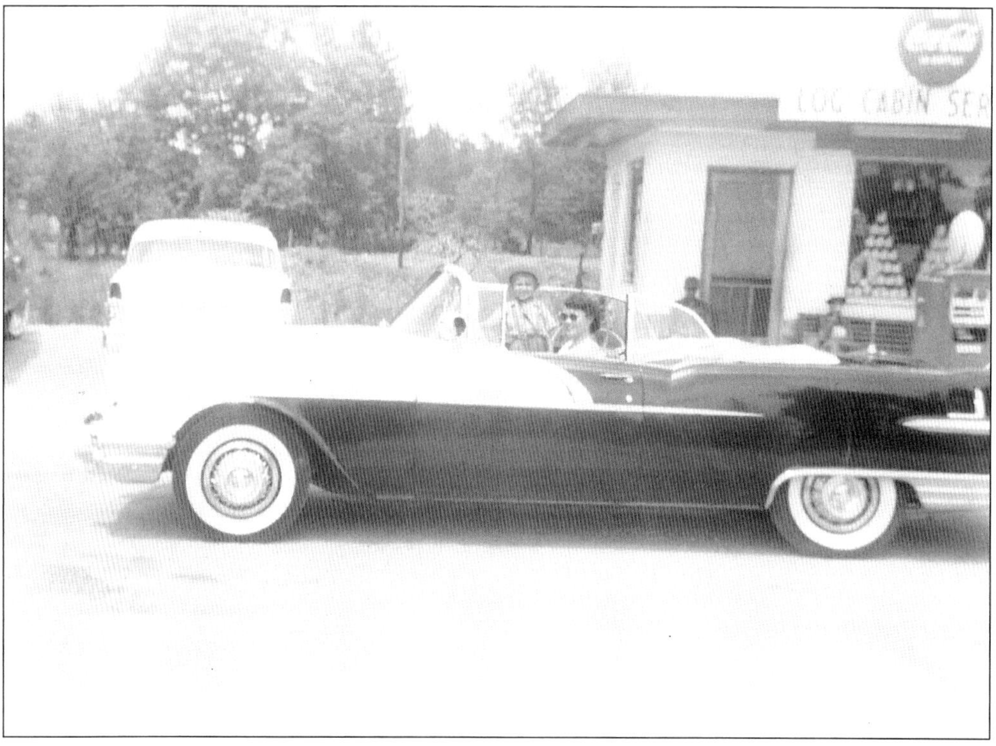

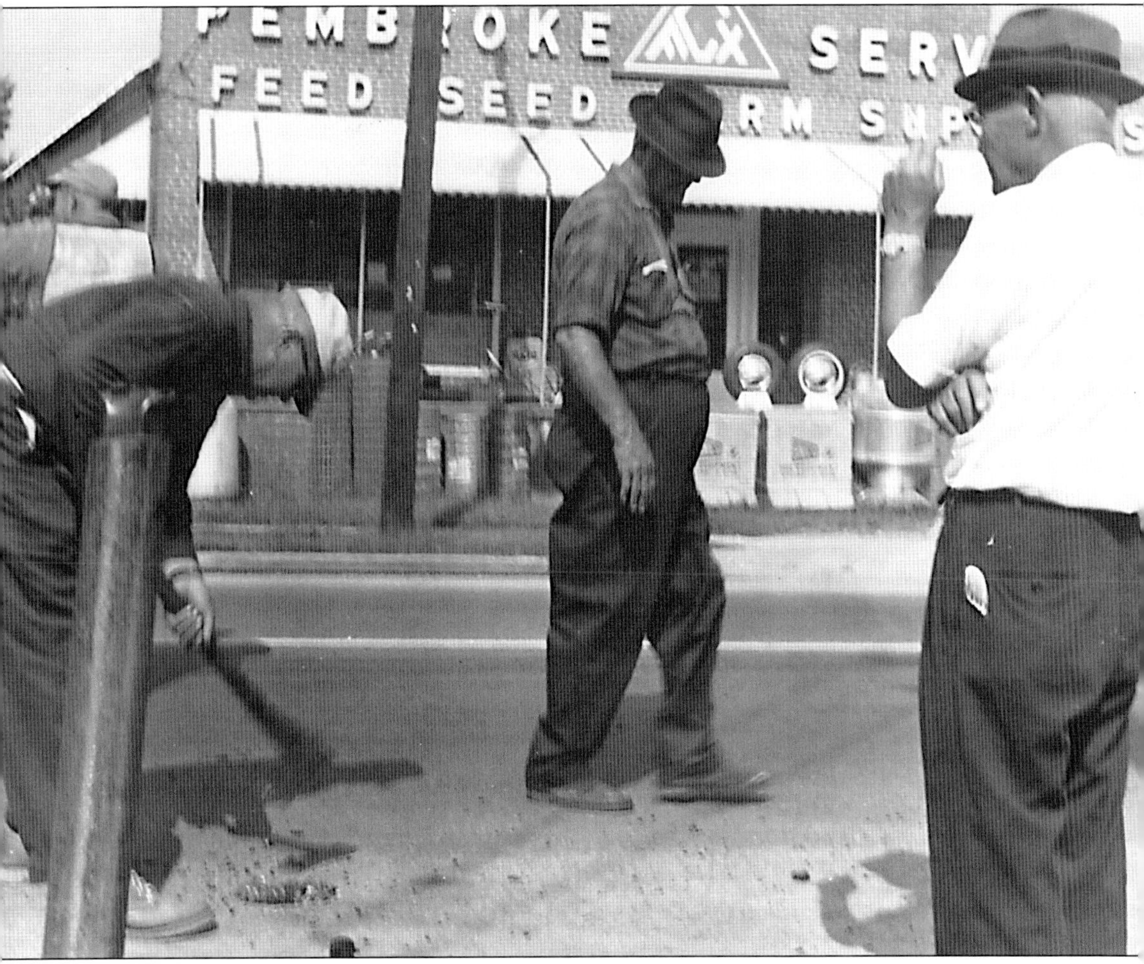

Mayor James C. "Sonny" Oxendine is shown in the 1960s overseeing street construction in front of the Pembroke FCX. The FCX later became Pembroke Home and Garden Supply.

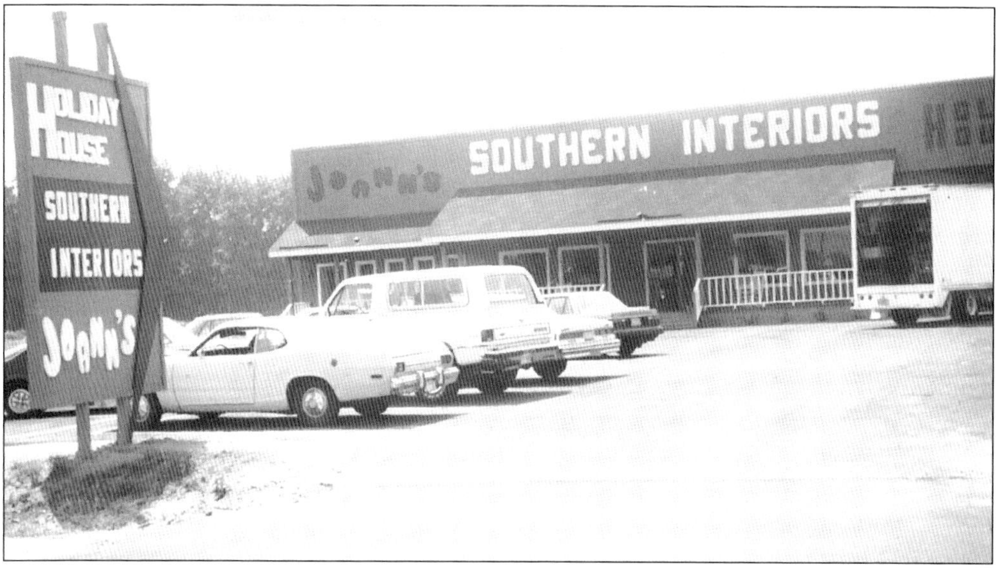

This is a view of Southern Interiors, JoAnn's, and Holiday House, which are all in one complex on Union Chapel Road. JoAnn's is now Native Herbs, and Holiday House is the headquarters for Pemberton Medical Supplies and Equipment, another business venture involving Charles Alton Maynor, the owner of Southern Interiors.

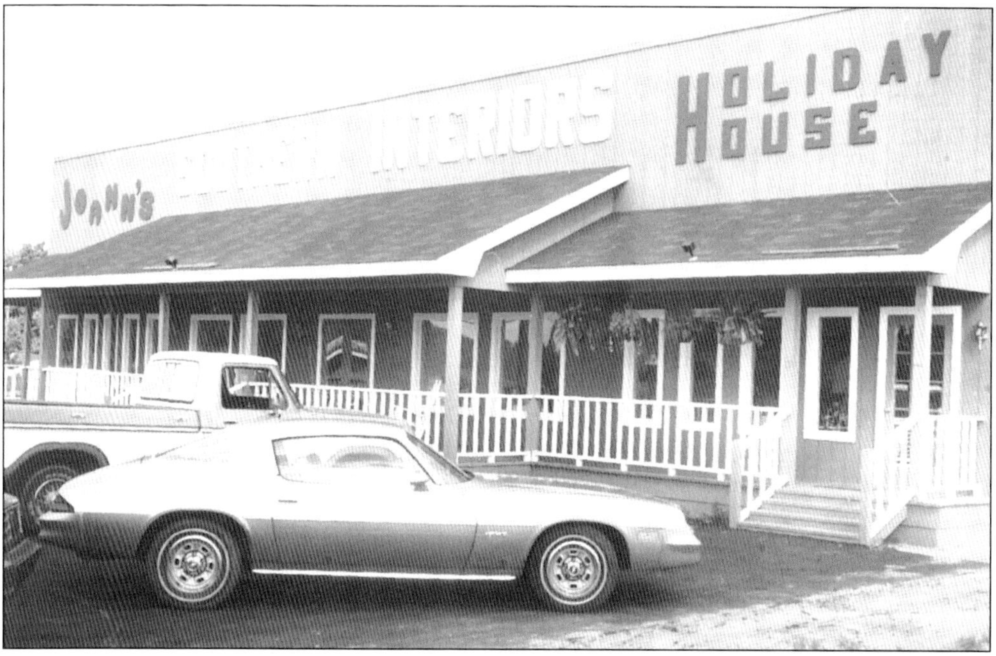

Southern Interiors, a Native American–owned business, specializes in interior decorating. It is owned and operated by Charles Alton and Sheila Maynor. The business moved to this new location from West Third Street in 1988. Southern Interiors is now located on Union Chapel Road.

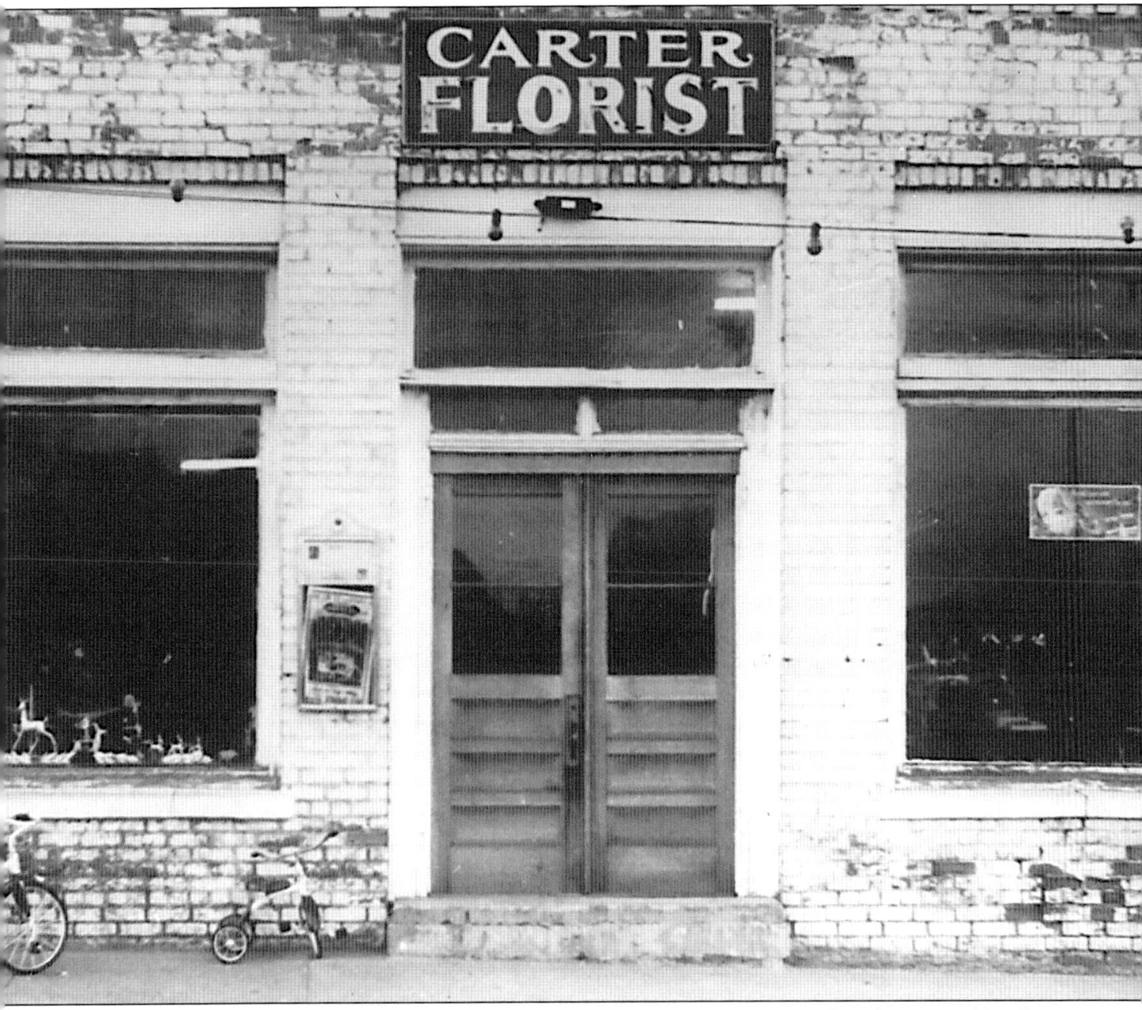

Carter's Florist, located in downtown Pembroke for many years, was owned and operated by the late Rose Carter in this location for 15 years. This photograph of her store was taken in 1953. When she vacated this building with her florist, Mrs. Carter opened a shop behind her house on Highway 711. Mrs. Carter also taught in the public schools and, after retirement, continued her floral business until her death in 1993.

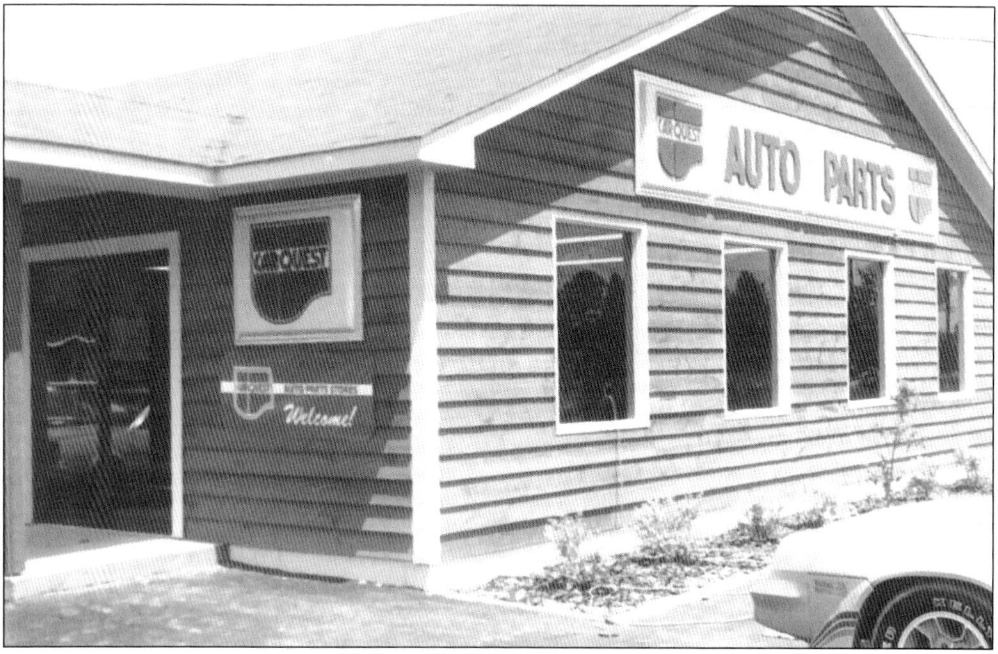

Carquest Auto Parts, located on West Third Street, is operated by Kelly Cummings. The business has moved to another location on West Third Street since this photograph was taken.

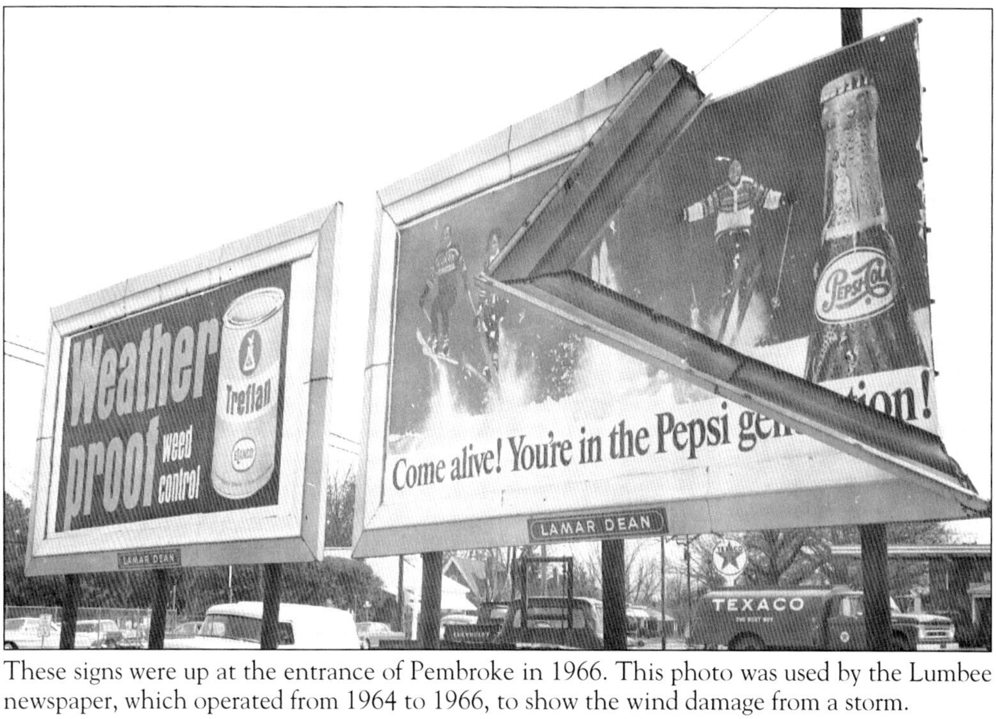

These signs were up at the entrance of Pembroke in 1966. This photo was used by the Lumbee newspaper, which operated from 1964 to 1966, to show the wind damage from a storm.

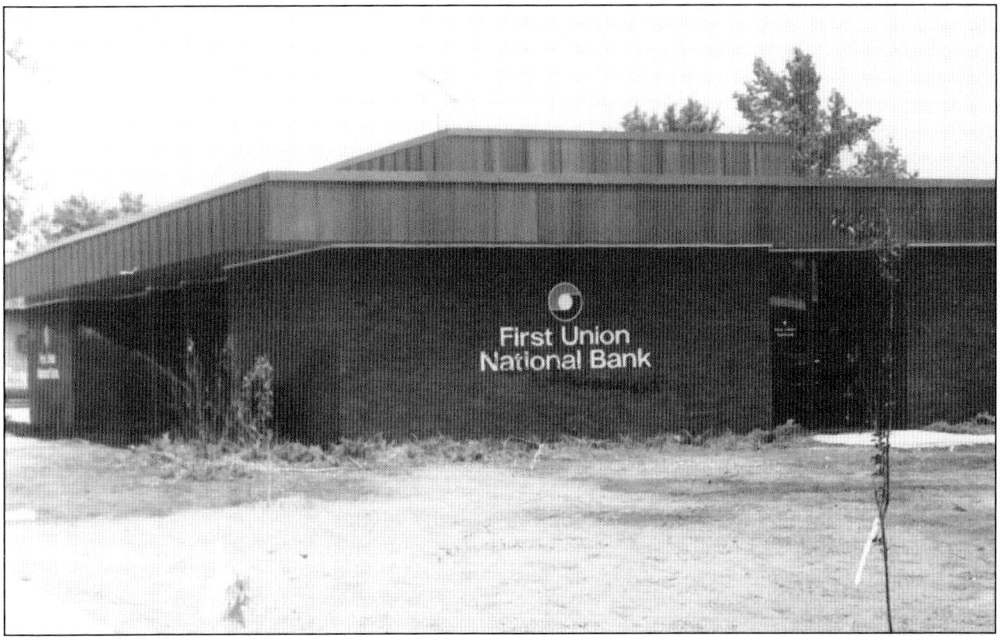

First Union National Bank, a longtime member of the Pembroke business community, is located on West Third Street. While there has not been a Lumbee president of the Pembroke Branch, several Lumbees serve on its board of directors.

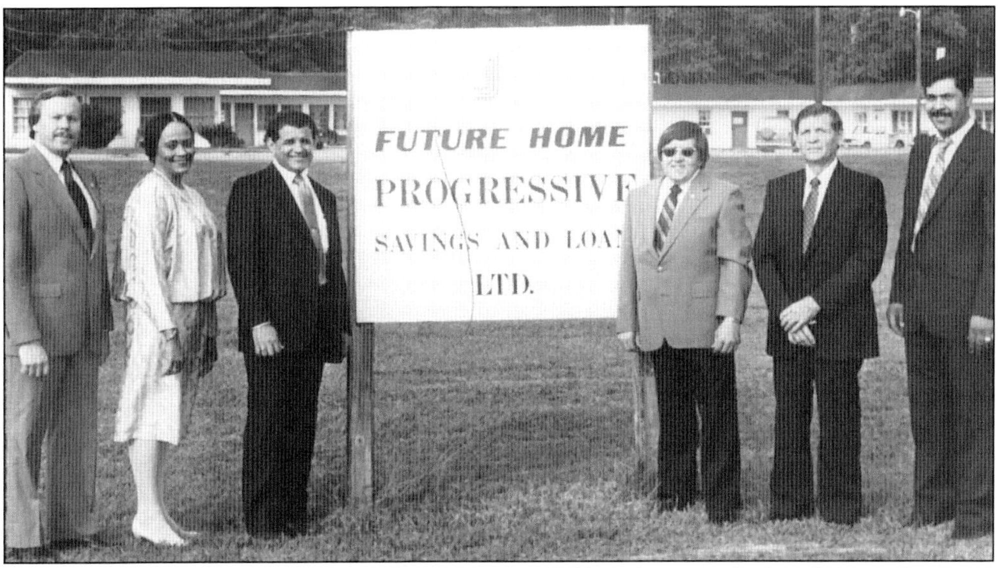

The Pembroke town manager, McDuffie Cummings (left), is shown with, from left to right, Betty Brooks; Dr. Jeff Collins; Mayor Milton Hunt; Jimmy Hedgepeth, the manager of Progressive Savings and Loan; and Harold Locklear. Progressive, located on West Third Street, became the third banking institution in Pembroke.

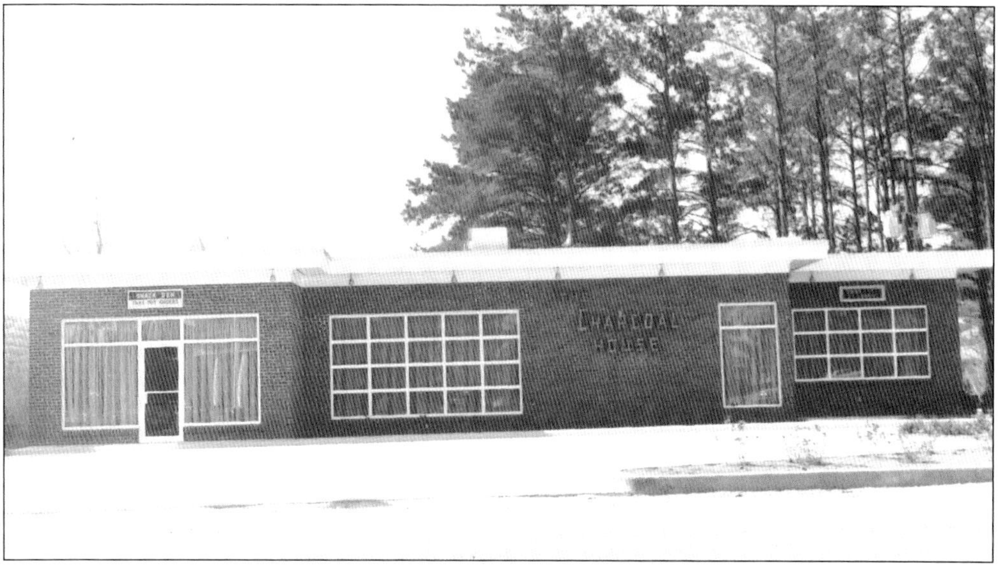

The Charcoal House was located across from the university in Pembroke. It was owned by Ancil Sanderson and managed by Hughes D. and Mary Lowry during the early 1960s. Following their years of management, the Charcoal House was subleased to nationally known singer Ronnie Dove. It was under his sublease that it was operated a very short time before being destroyed by fire.

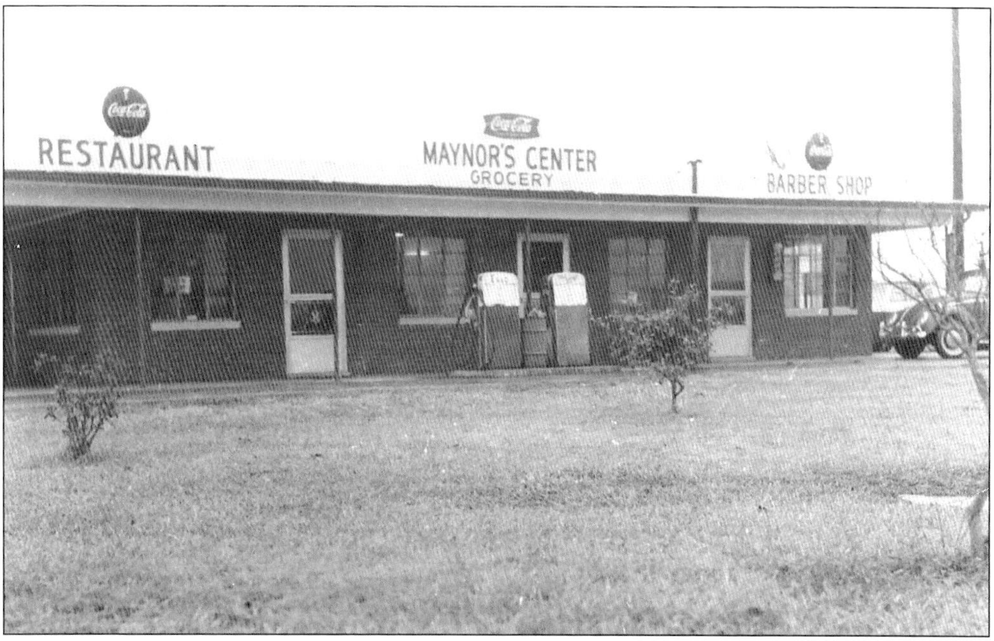

Maynor's Center is located in the Union Chapel community at the intersection of Union Chapel Road and Highway 72. In the 1960s, Maynor's Center included a Native American–owned restaurant, grocery store, and barbershop.

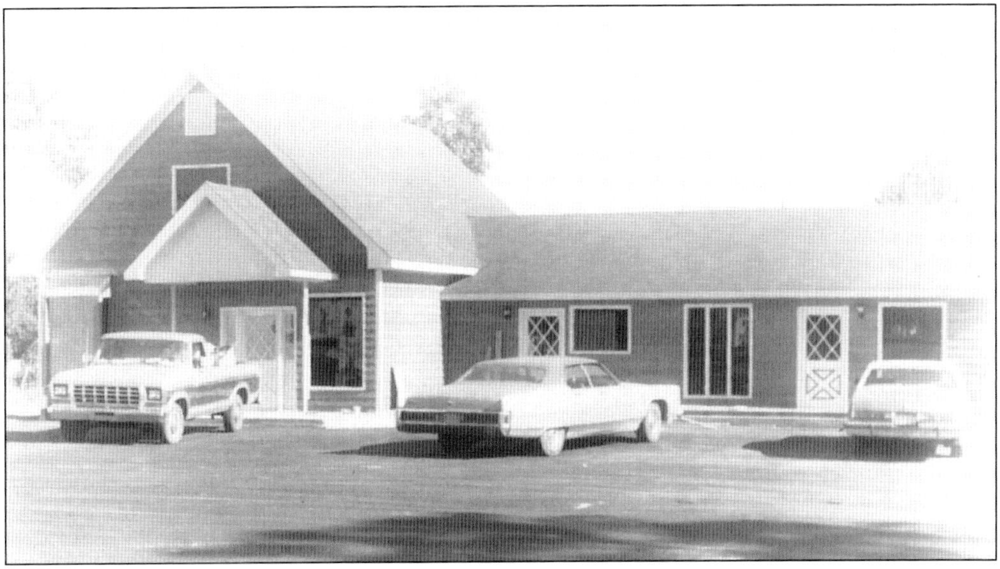

Lorraine's Clothing on Union Chapel Road was constructed by Mack Locklear of Mack's Construction, one of the leading construction contractors in the state. Lorraine's Clothing was operated by Mack's wife, Lorraine Locklear.

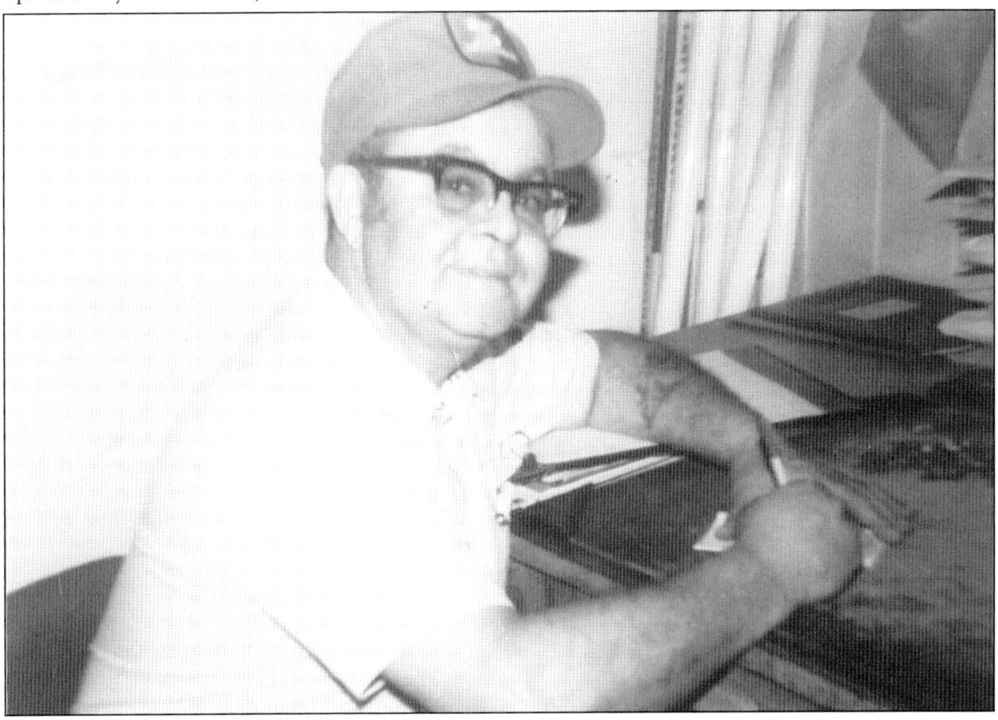

Vardell Ransom is shown in his office at the Road Runner Service Station, located across from the Pembroke Town Hall. Mr. Ransom owned and operated this service station until his retirement. He was born on February 25, 1929, and died on July 29, 1997. In addition to his mechanical ability, Mr. Ransom was widely known and admired for his gifted biblical teaching. He was an active member of New Hope Church, where he taught a Bible class for many years. The Road Runner is still operated by his son, Kent Ransom.

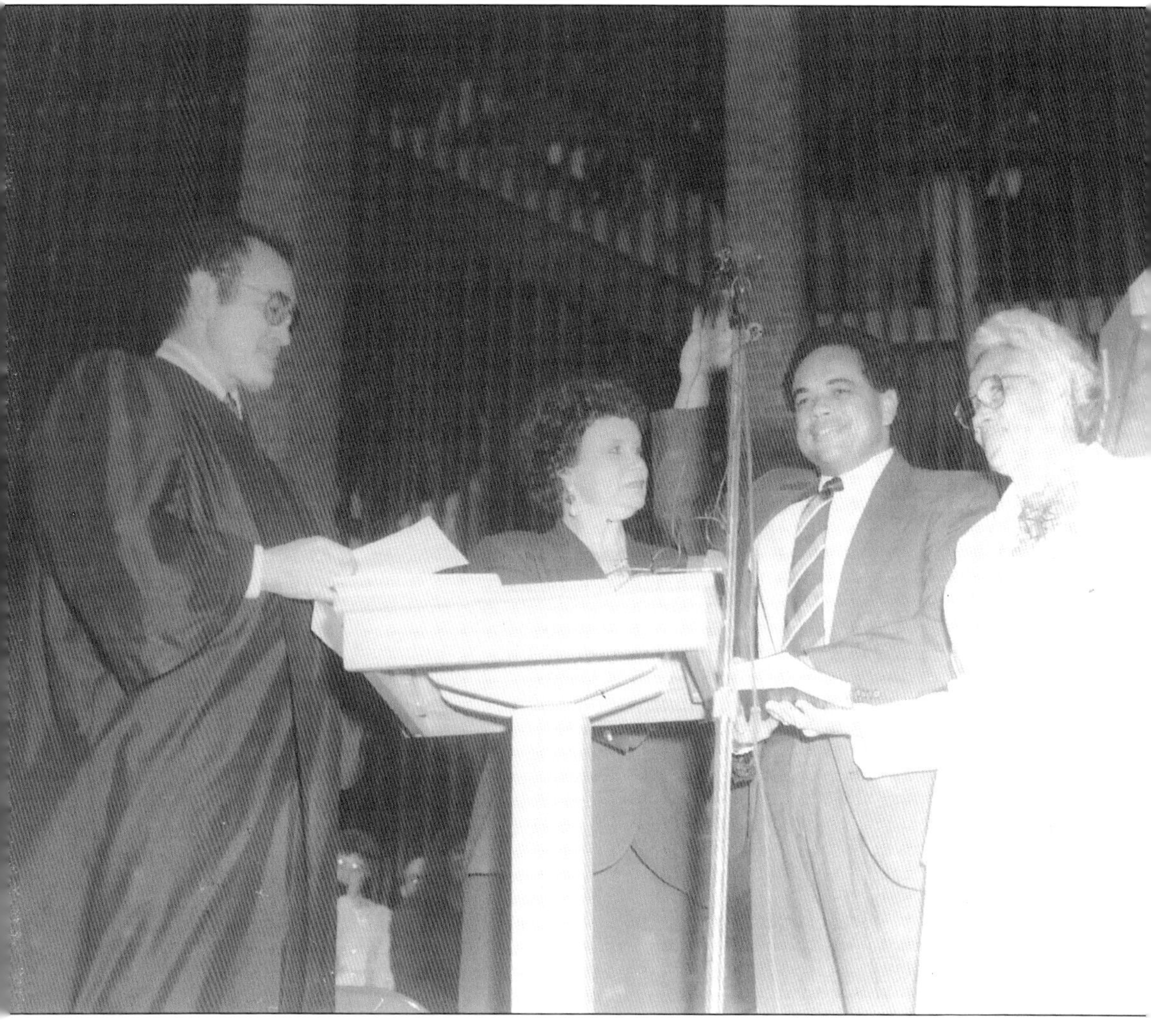

This historic photo was taken in 1994 at the swearing-in ceremony for the first Native American sheriff in Robeson County. Shown, from left to right, are the Honorable Dexter Brooks, who administered the oath of office; Mrs. Glenn Maynor; Glenn Maynor, the high sheriff of Robeson County; and the sheriff's mother, Mrs. Myrtle Maynor.

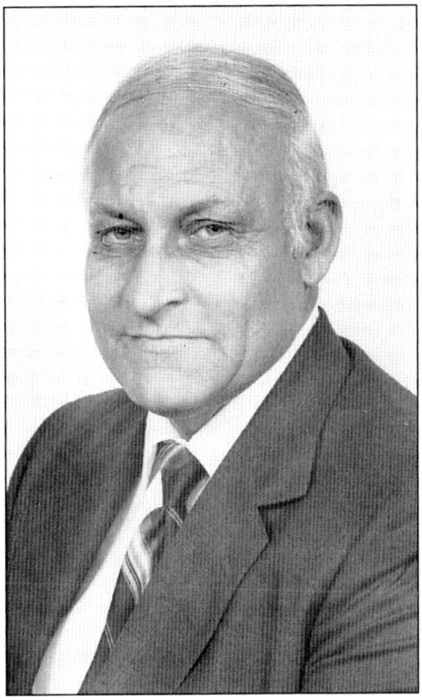

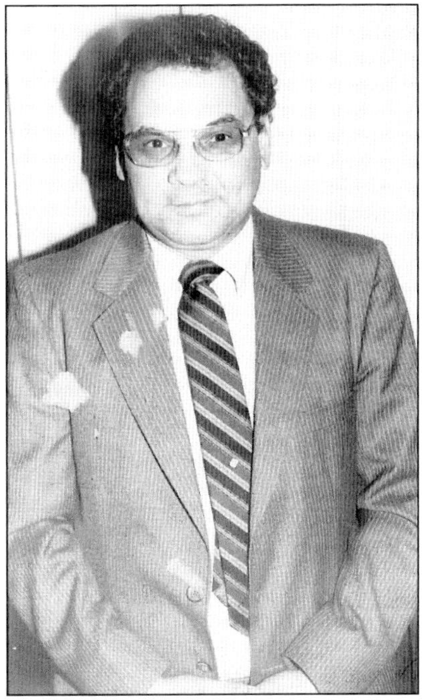

Left: Joel Garth Locklear, the son of the first Native American mayor, Rev. C.E. Locklear, worked for many years with the Robeson County Sheriff's Department. He is presently employed as an investigator for the Robeson County Public Defender's Office. He also operates a private investigator's business part time. Locklear is the chairman of the Indian Honor Association and serves as an elected member to the North Carolina Commission of Indian Affairs. *Right:* Henry Ward Oxendine was the first Lumbee to serve in the North Carolina General Assembly. He was appointed in 1973 to replace the late Rep. Frank White. Representative Oxendine served two terms in the North Carolina House of Representatives. He is a licensed attorney with the State of North Carolina and serves as assistant to the Robeson County District Attorney.

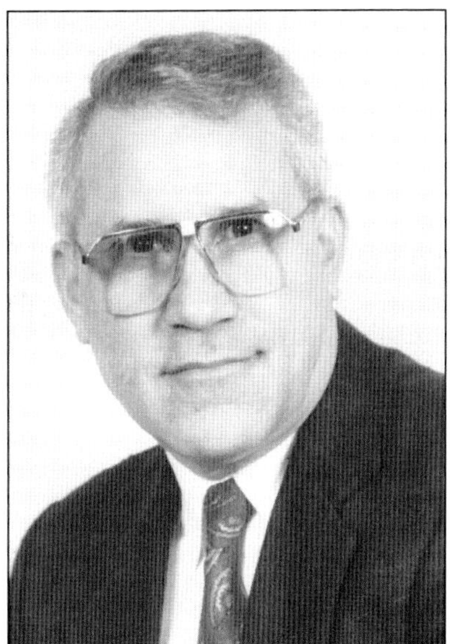

Rep. Ronnie Sutton serves in the North Carolina General Assembly, representing District 85, commonly referred to as the "Indian District." He is the only Native American serving in the state legislature. An attorney practicing on Union Chapel Road, Pembroke, Rep. Sutton is also retired from the United States Navy where he earned the rank of Commander.

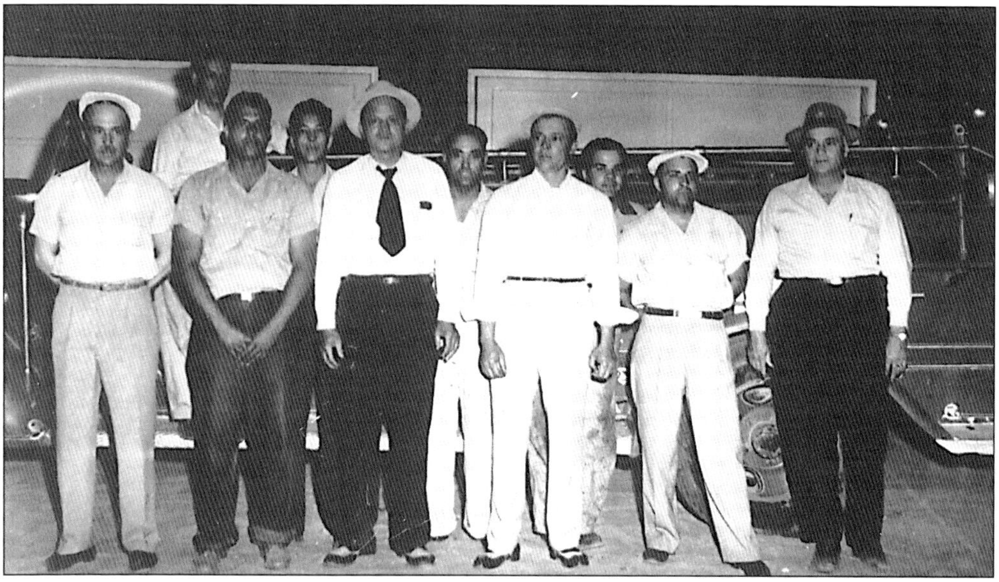

Shown here are early members of the Pembroke Volunteer Fire Department. They are, from left to right, as follows: (front row) Plummer Locklear, Robert McGirt, Theodore Maynor, unidentified, Governor Barnes, and Harry West Locklear; (back row) J.W. Chavis, Calvin Chavis, Fred Godwin, and Simeon Oxendine.

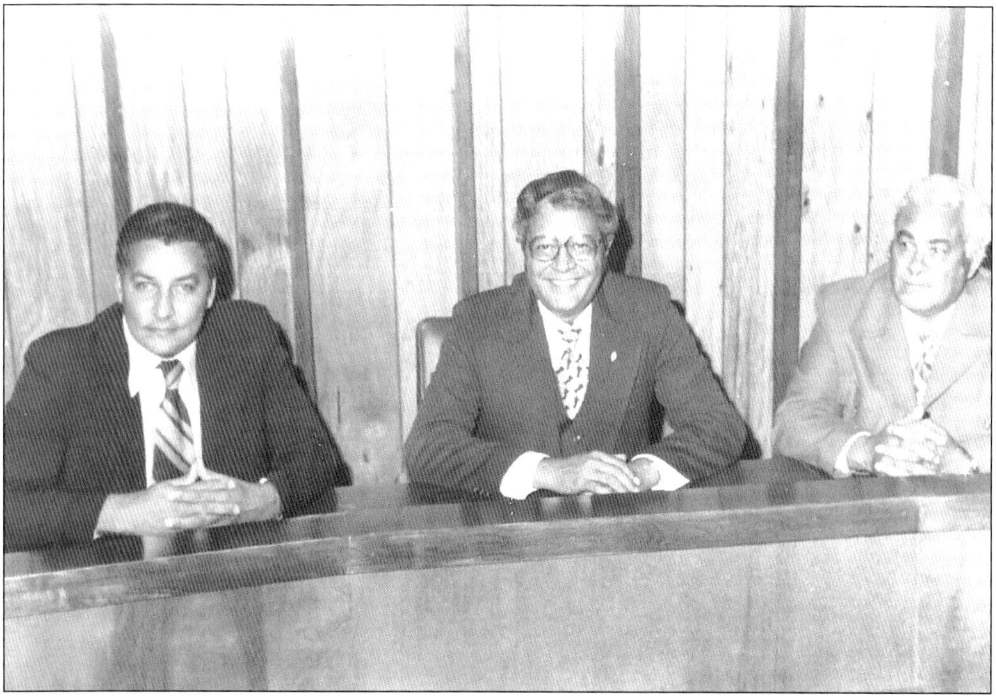

Shown, from left to right, are Roderick Glenn Locklear, Mayor James A. Jacobs, and Councilman Sam Dial. Dial was called the "Father of Public Housing," and Dial Terrace, one of five developments of the Pembroke Housing Authority, is named in his honor. Dial also served on the town council. Locklear is a board member with Lumbee Regional Development Association and is employed with the Social Security Administration in Washington, D.C.

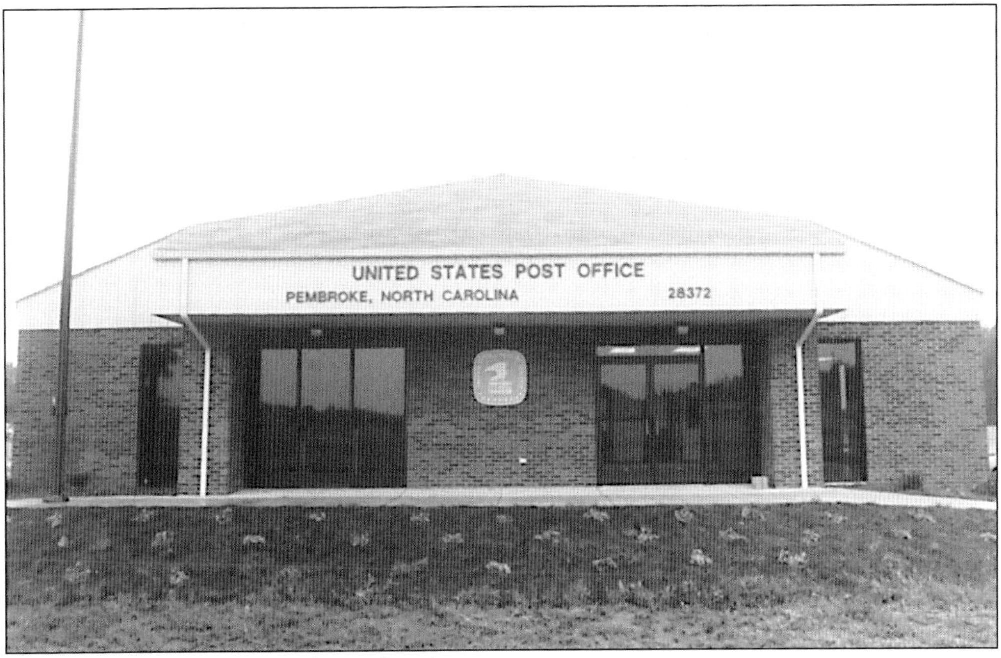

The Pembroke Post Office is located at the Colony Plaza, across from the corporate offices of Lumbee Guaranty Bank. John H. Sampson (right) was the first Native American postmaster. He was followed by Dosey Chavis, a Lumbee. The postmaster now is Gerald Lee, a non-Native American.

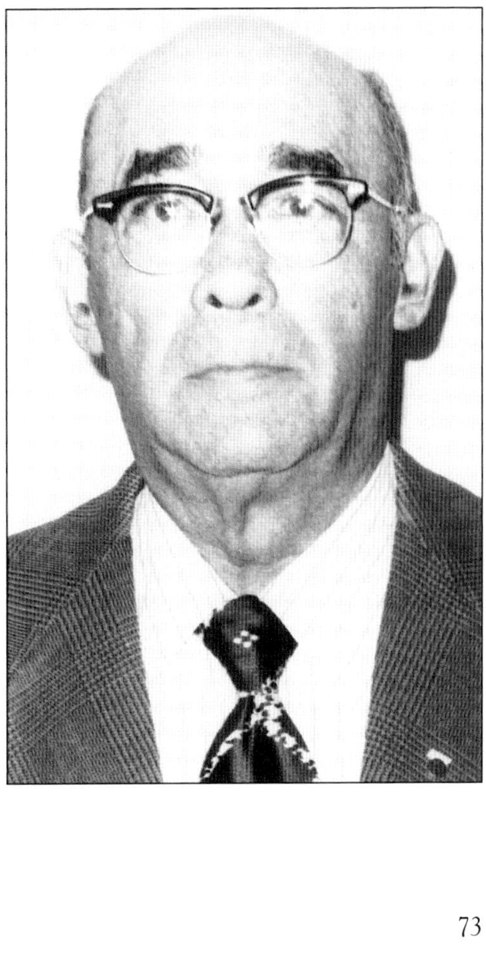

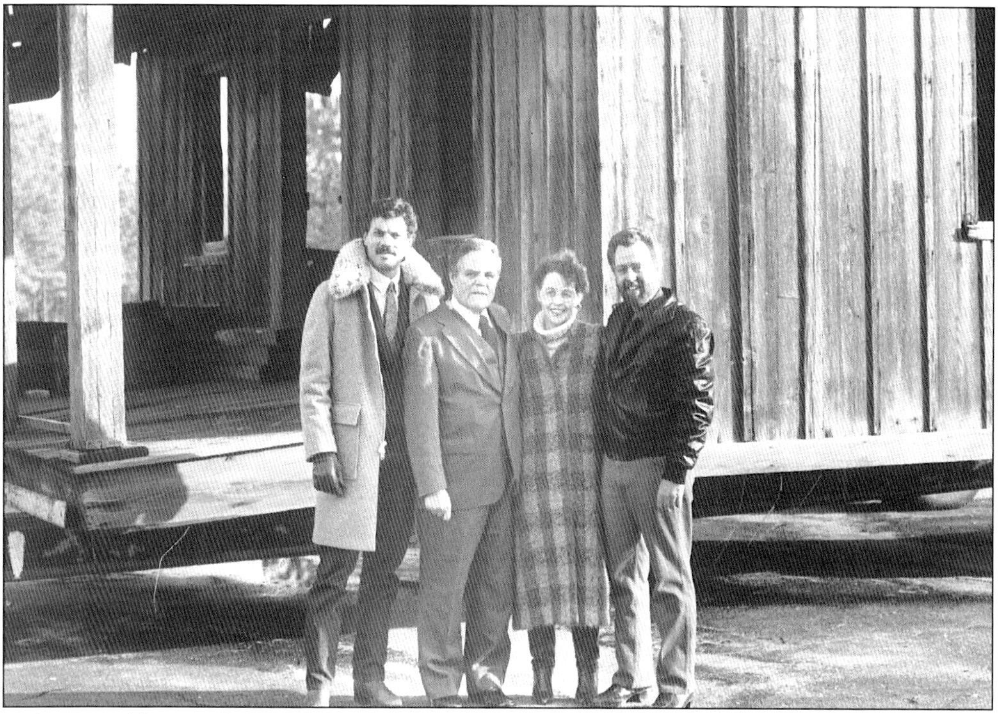

Robert Locklear, Adolph Dial, and Helen Schirbeck are shown at the North Carolina Indian Cultural Center after the Henry Berry Lowrie House had been relocated there for the purposes of renovation. Schirbeck was the director of the North Carolina Indian Cultural Center at the time.

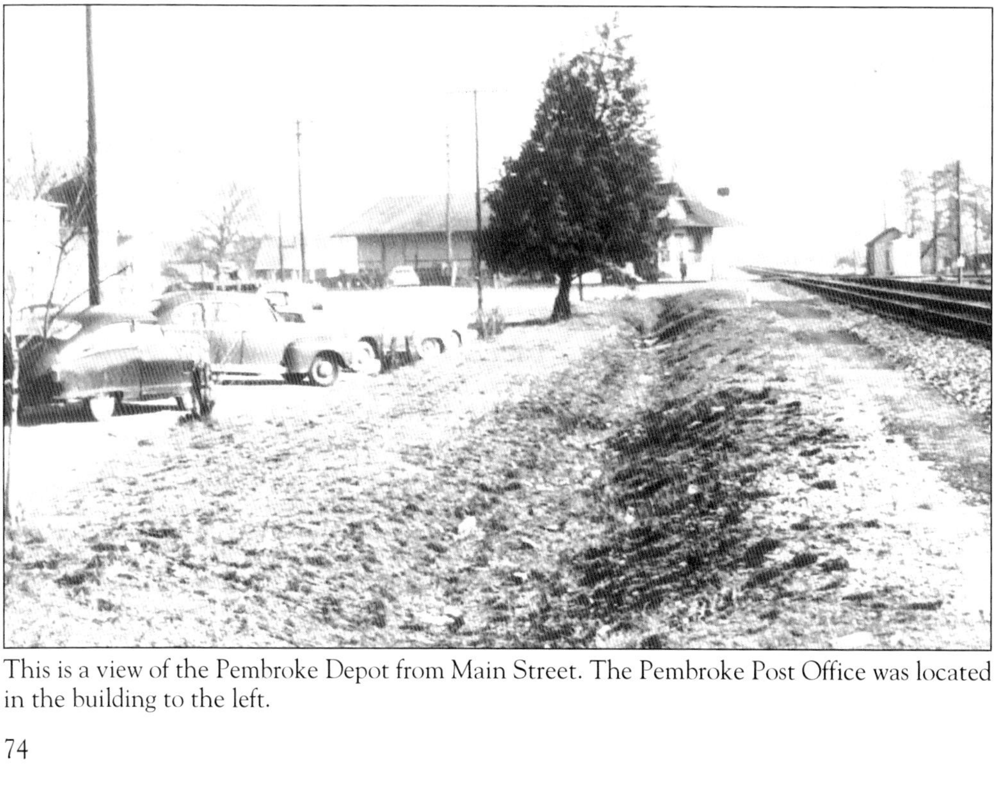

This is a view of the Pembroke Depot from Main Street. The Pembroke Post Office was located in the building to the left.

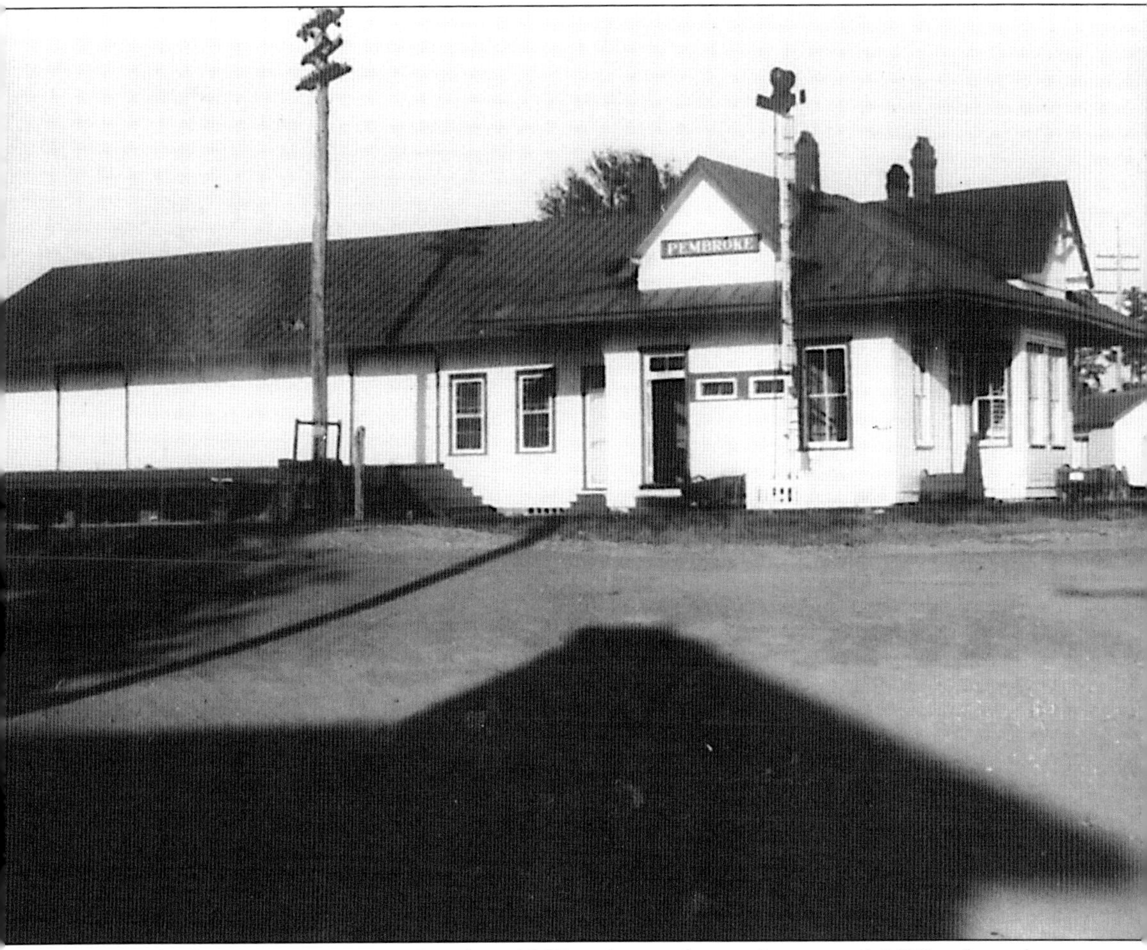

The Pembroke Depot was erected in late 1885 and served as a depot until 1975, when the railroads no longer used Pembroke as a stop for passengers.

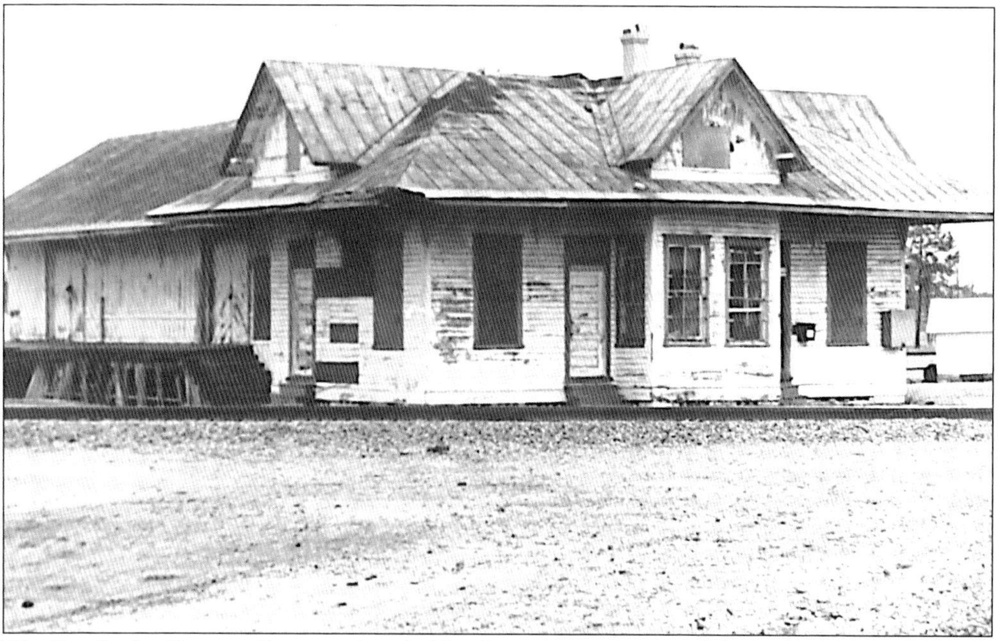

The Pembroke Historic Society, founded by Bruce Barton, moved the Pembroke Depot from its original location for the purposes of renovating this historic building. Unfortunately, the building was destroyed by fire shortly after it was relocated in 1987. Below, home movers are shown relocating the Pembroke Depot.

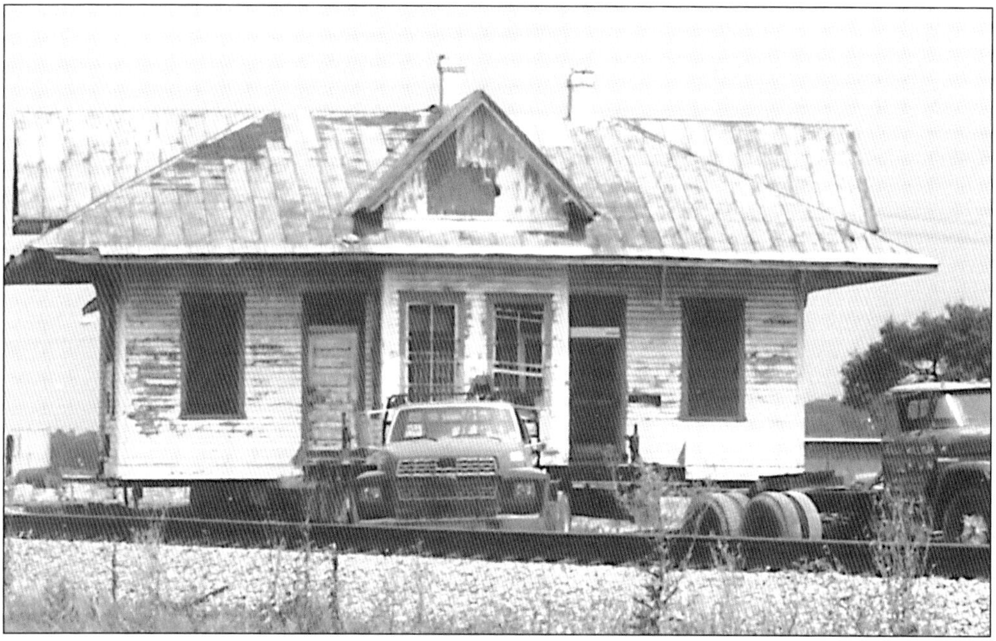

Four

Schools and Education

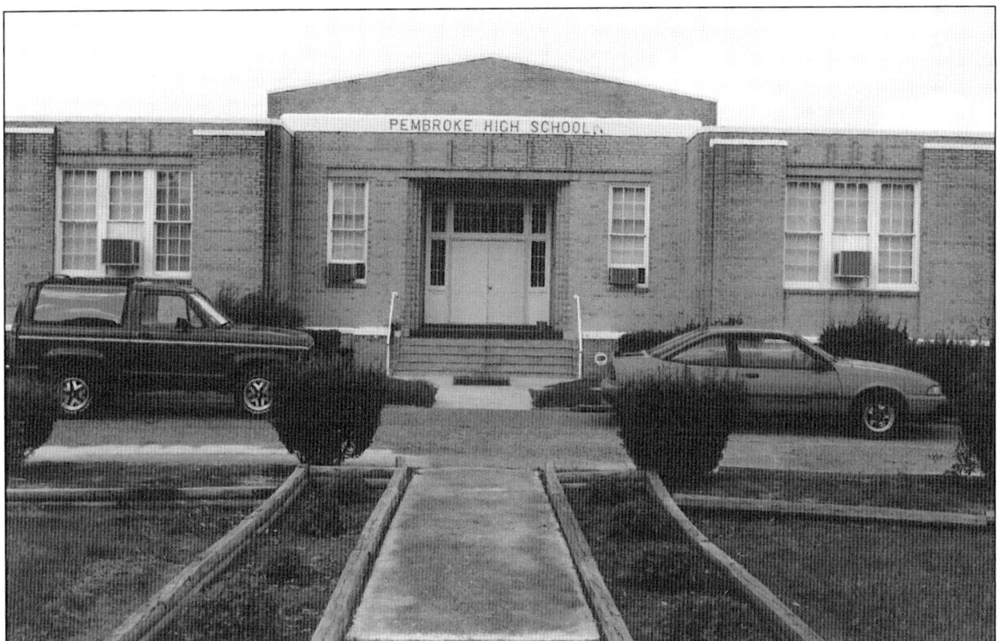

Pembroke High School was the first high school for Native Americans in North Carolina. It was built in 1939 as part of the Federal Works Program under President Franklin D. Roosevelt. It was Pembroke High School from 1939 until 1967, when Pembroke Senior High was built on a new site. The original school building is now on the North Carolina Registry as a historic site. The building was renovated and now houses the Indian Education Program of the Public Schools of Robeson County. Mr. Elmer T. Lowry was the school's first principal and served until 1967. The site has been used as Pembroke Junior High School and was eventually abandoned by the county board of education. It was preserved and restored by Indian Solidarity, Inc., a nonprofit corporation. The school was leased to the organization for $1 per year and eventually returned to the public school system.

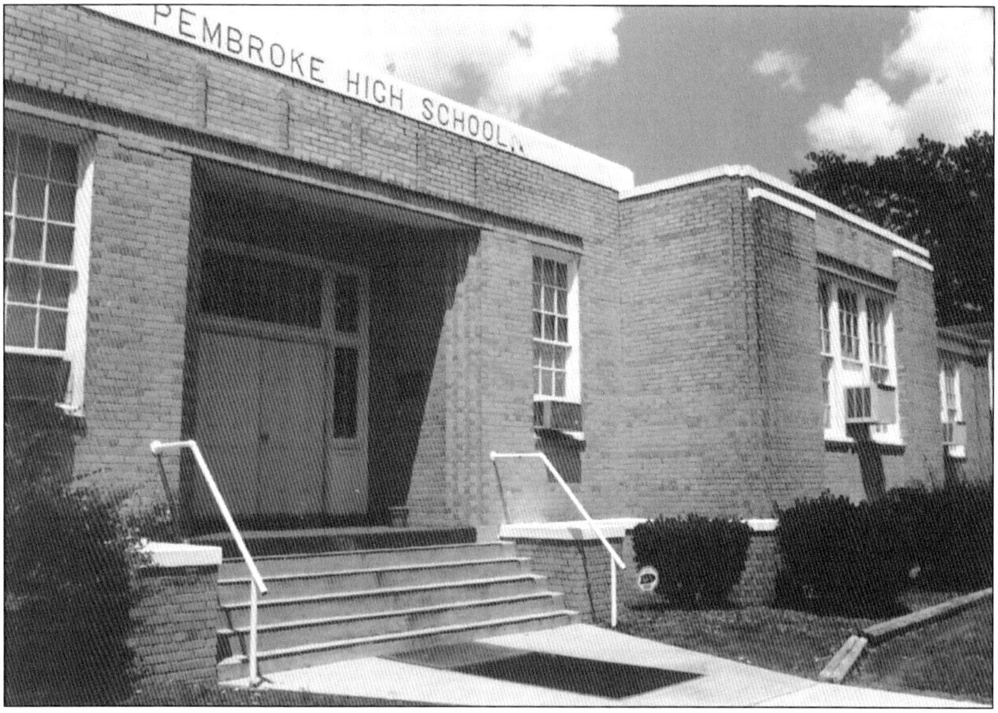

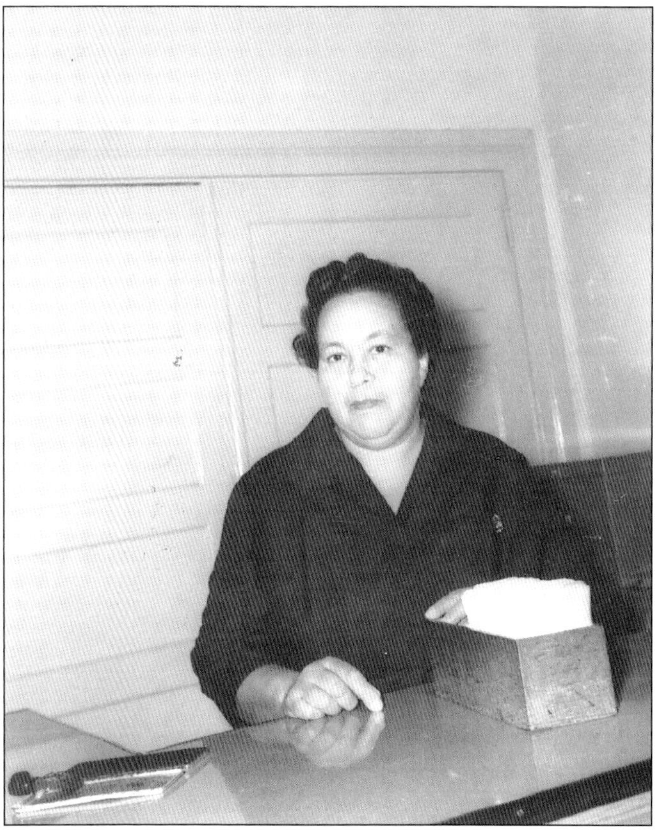

This is a closer view of Pembroke High School following its renovation and distinction as a North Carolina historic site.

In this 1961 photograph, Mrs. Ruby C. Dial is shown in the library of Pembroke High School, where she served for more than 25 years. She was well loved and respected by the students, for she taught them to appreciate and to care for library books.

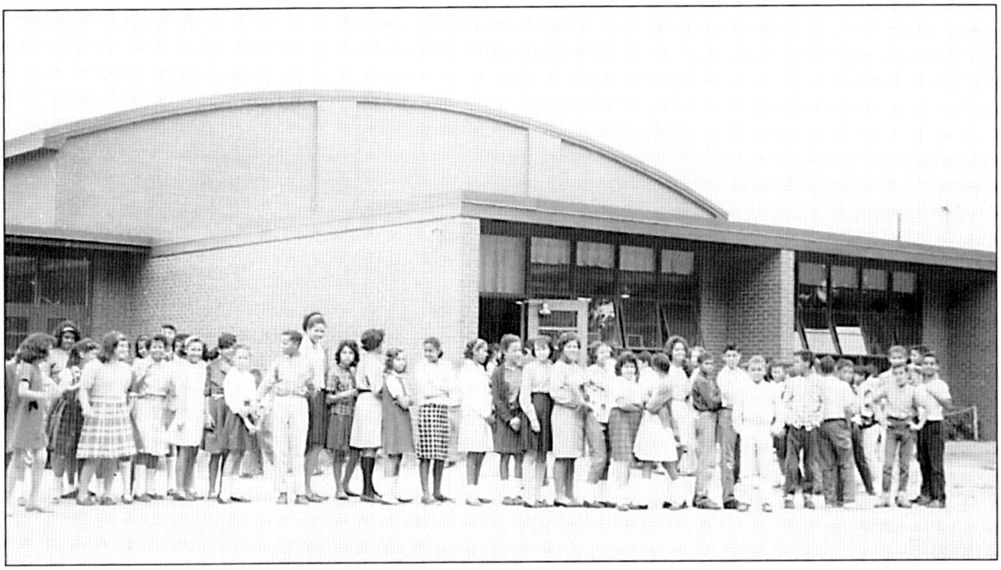

This is a photo of the Adrian B. McRae Gymnasium of Pembroke High School, the first Native American four-year high school in the United States.

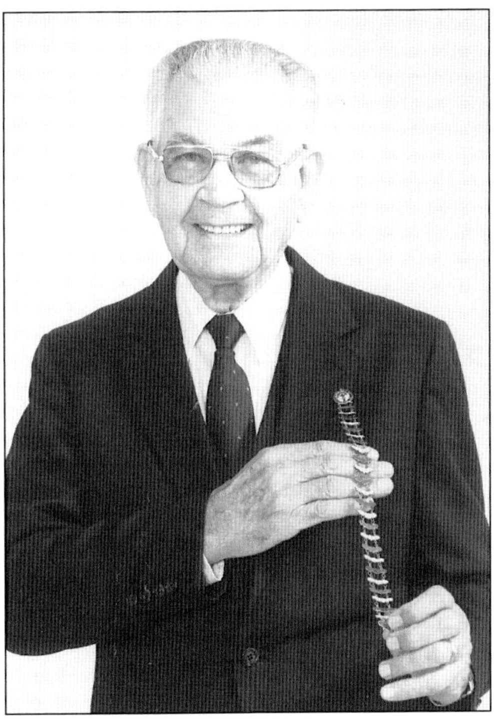

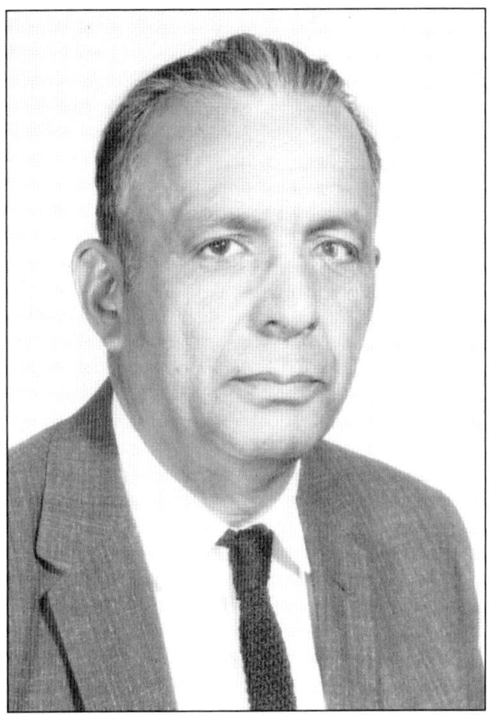

Left: Earlie Maynor was a schoolteacher and served as mayor of Pembroke from 1967 to 1973. After his retirement from the public school system, he spent his time volunteering in local schools and encouraged children to attend Sunday school. Maynor had 30 years of perfect attendance in Sunday school when he died. *Right:* Elmer T. Lowry of the Hopewell Community served as principal of the first Indian High School, Pembroke High, from 1940 until his retirement in 1964. The school was established in 1939, and J.R. Lowry served as principal the first year.

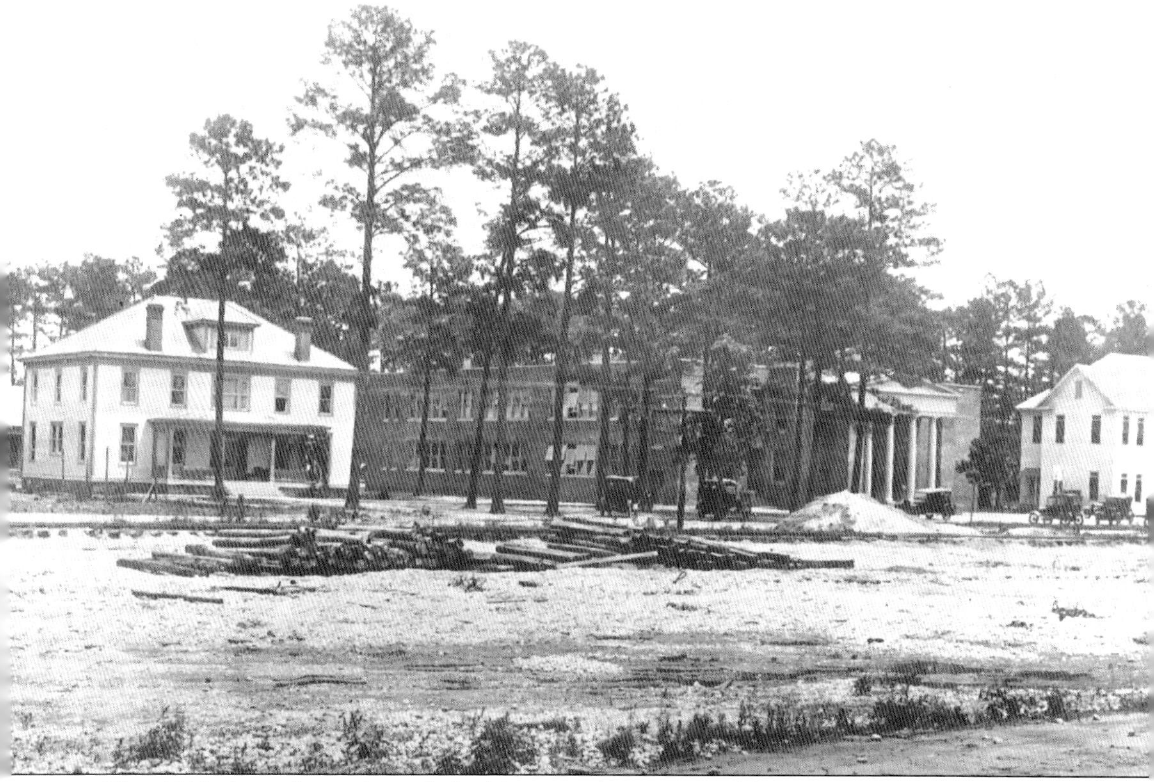

This 1925 photo shows the early buildings on the campus of the University of North Carolina at Pembroke; the first dormitory is on the left, and Old Main, the first brick structure, and the high school are on the right.

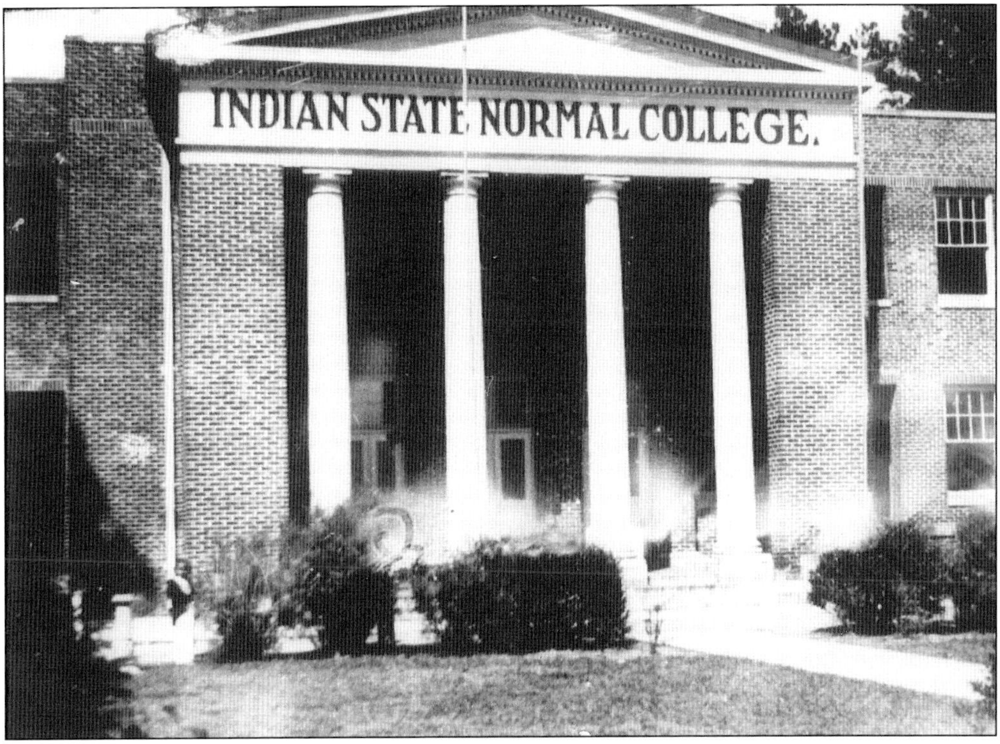

This is a photo of Old Main when the university was called Indian State Normal College.

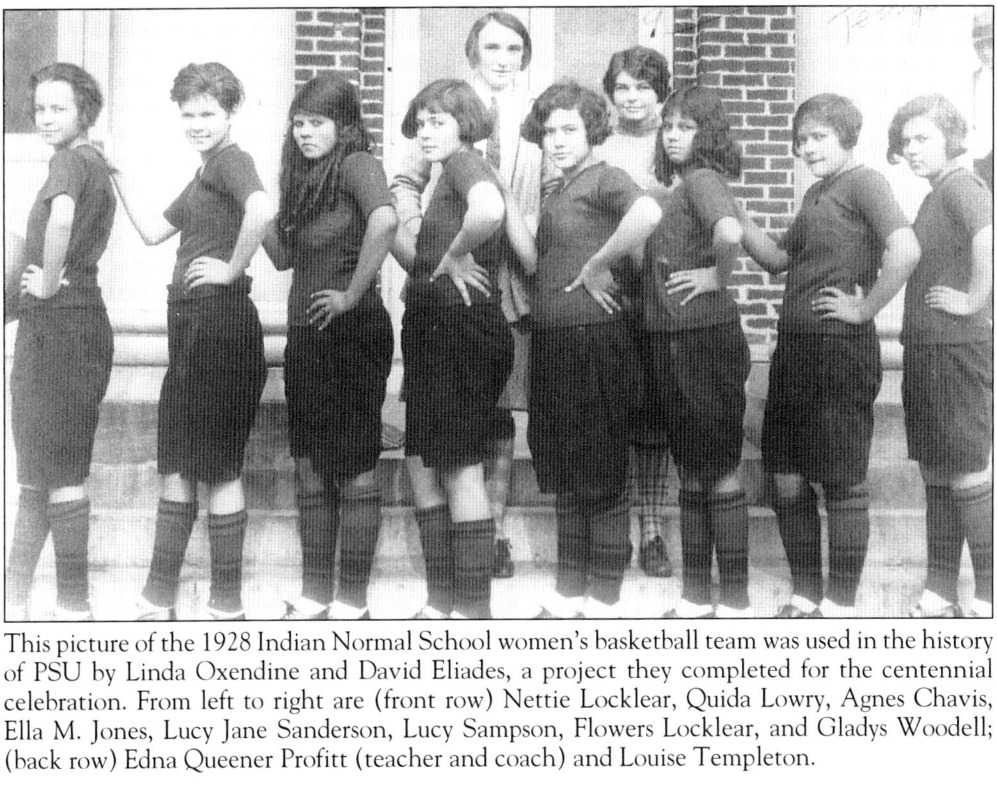

This picture of the 1928 Indian Normal School women's basketball team was used in the history of PSU by Linda Oxendine and David Eliades, a project they completed for the centennial celebration. From left to right are (front row) Nettie Locklear, Quida Lowry, Agnes Chavis, Ella M. Jones, Lucy Jane Sanderson, Lucy Sampson, Flowers Locklear, and Gladys Woodell; (back row) Edna Queener Profitt (teacher and coach) and Louise Templeton.

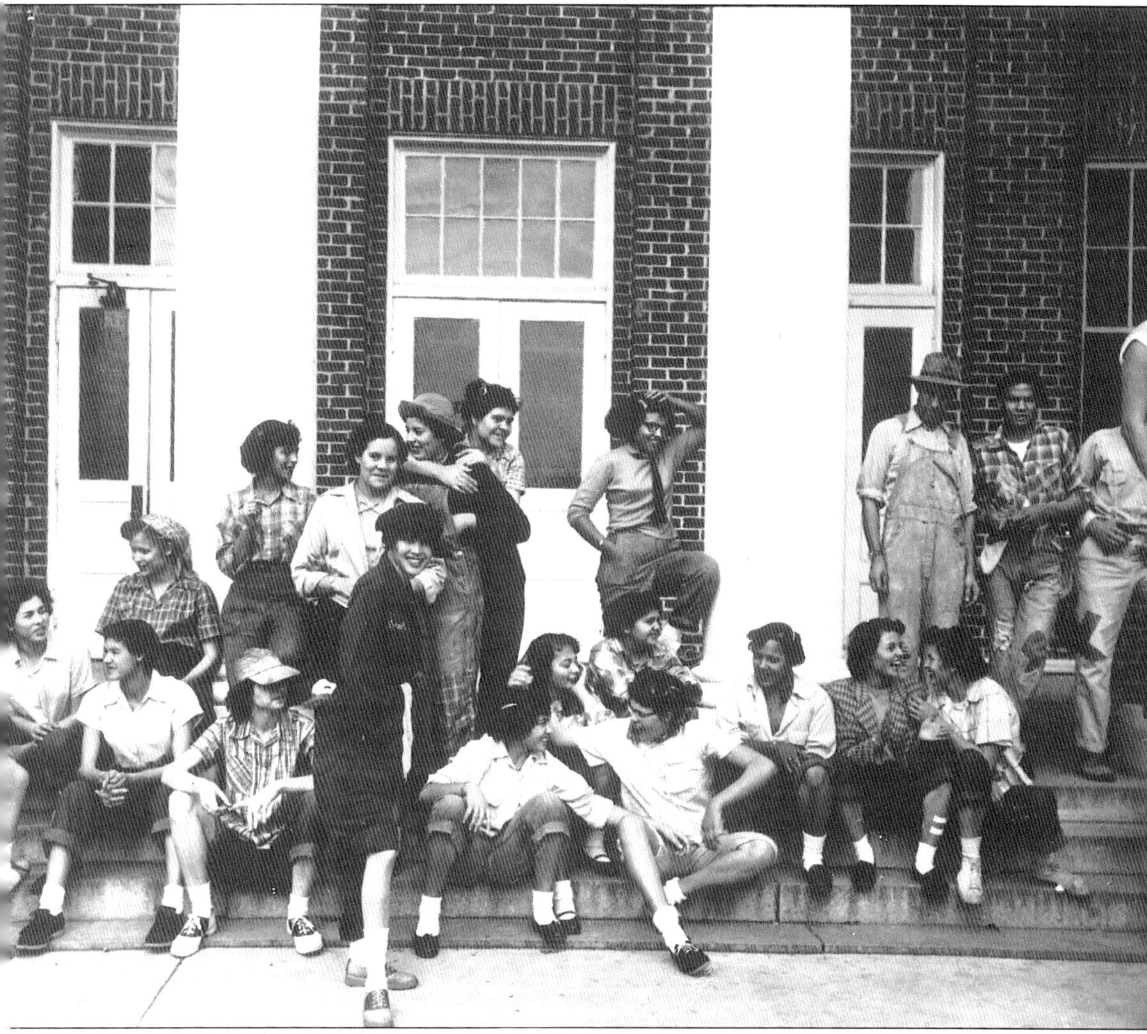

A group of students are shown here on the steps of Old Main on the campus of the University of North Carolina at Pembroke in 1954.

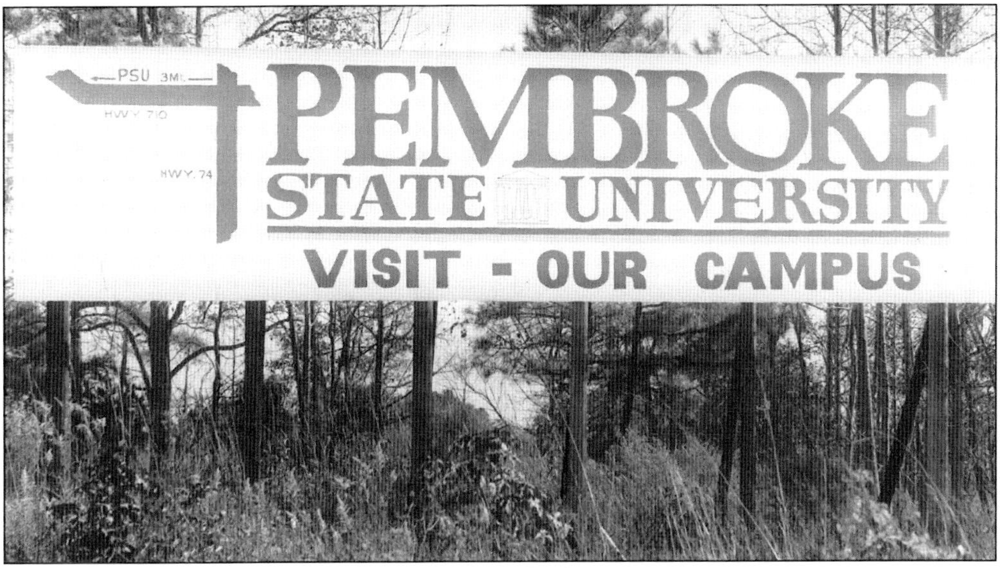

This sign welcomed visitors to the campus of Pembroke State University.

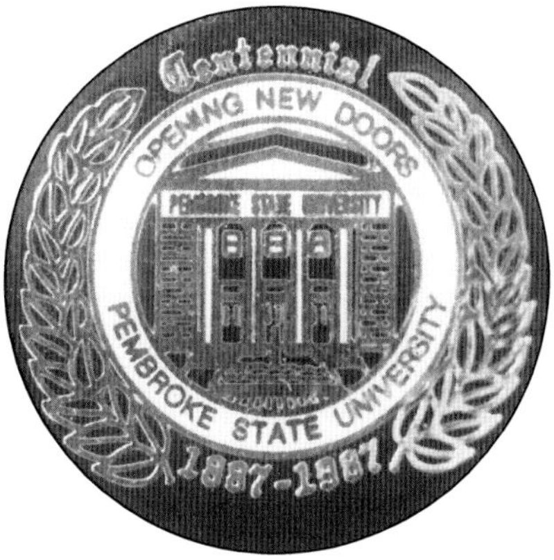

Dr. English E. Jones (left), the first Native American president of Pembroke State College, is shown here with Eugene Locklear, who owned and operated 5-G's Manufacturing. Jones became president in 1960. He retired from that institution in 1979 after it was renamed Pembroke State University. Jones has the distinction of being the first Native American to serve as the head of a state institution of higher learning.

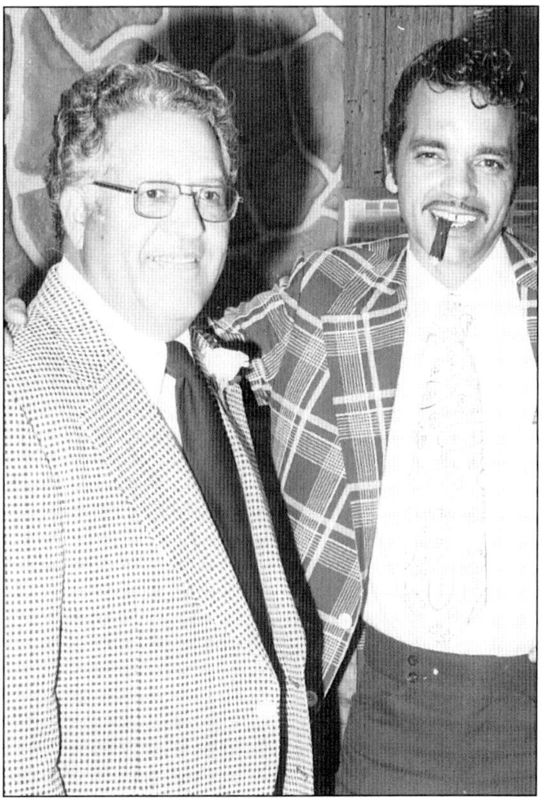

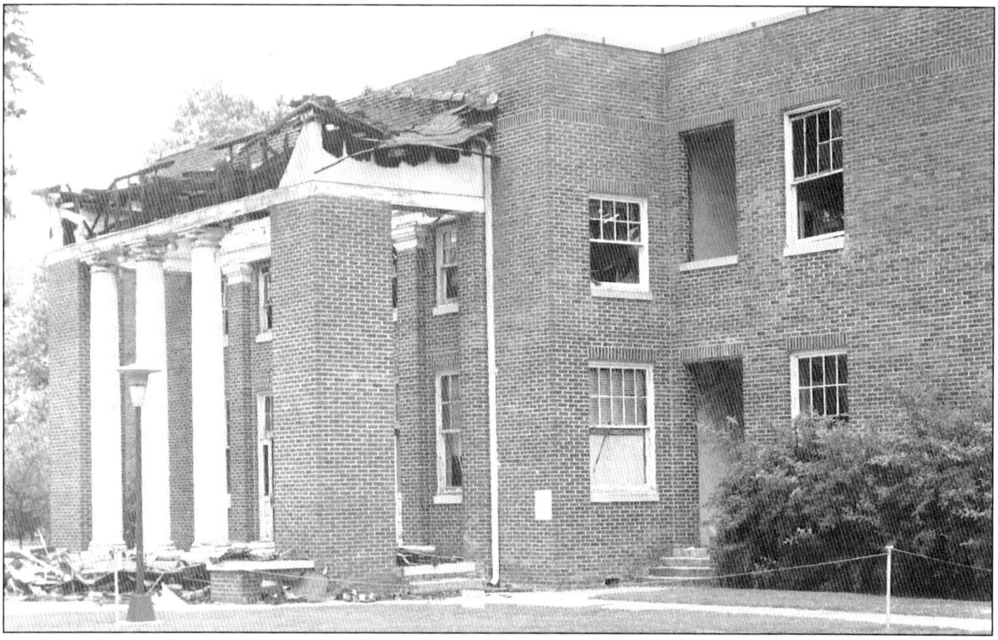

By 1978, Old Main shows the effects of years of neglect. This photo was taken after the fire that gutted the inside of the building and left only the outer walls standing.

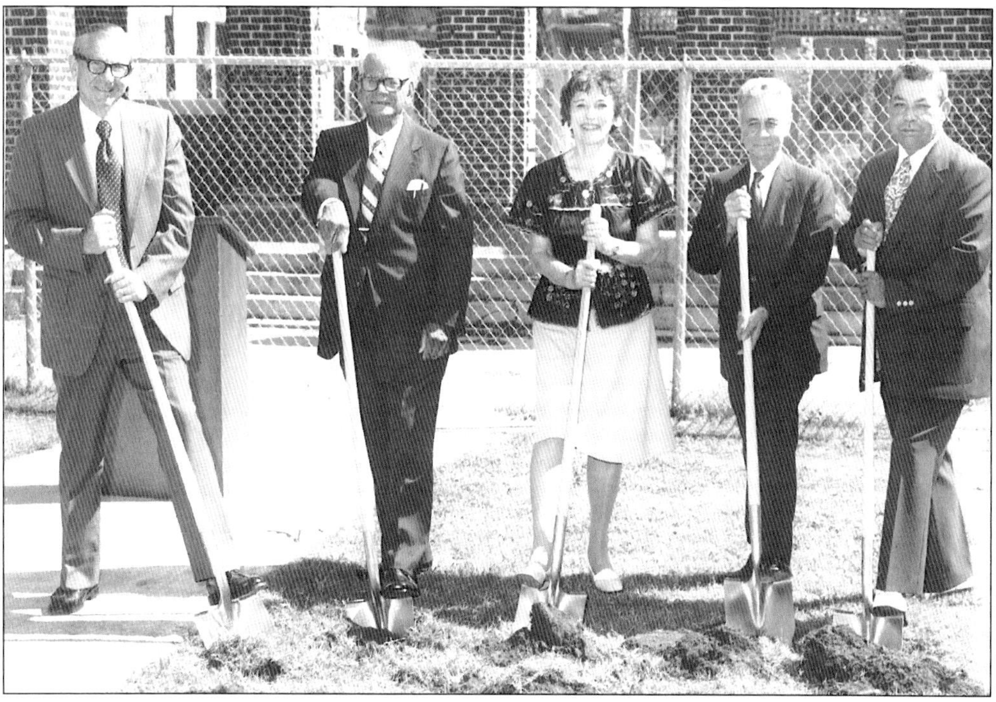

Groundbreaking ceremonies were held in 1979 for the $1.6-million reconstruction of the Old Main building at Pembroke State University. Pictured, from left to right, are Leroy Marks of Laurinburg, chairman of the PSU board of trustees; Clifton Oxendine, Reba Lowry, and James Jacobs, all of Pembroke and PSU professors emeritus; and John Robert Jones of Pembroke, chairman of the Old Main Commission, formed to save the building from being demolished.

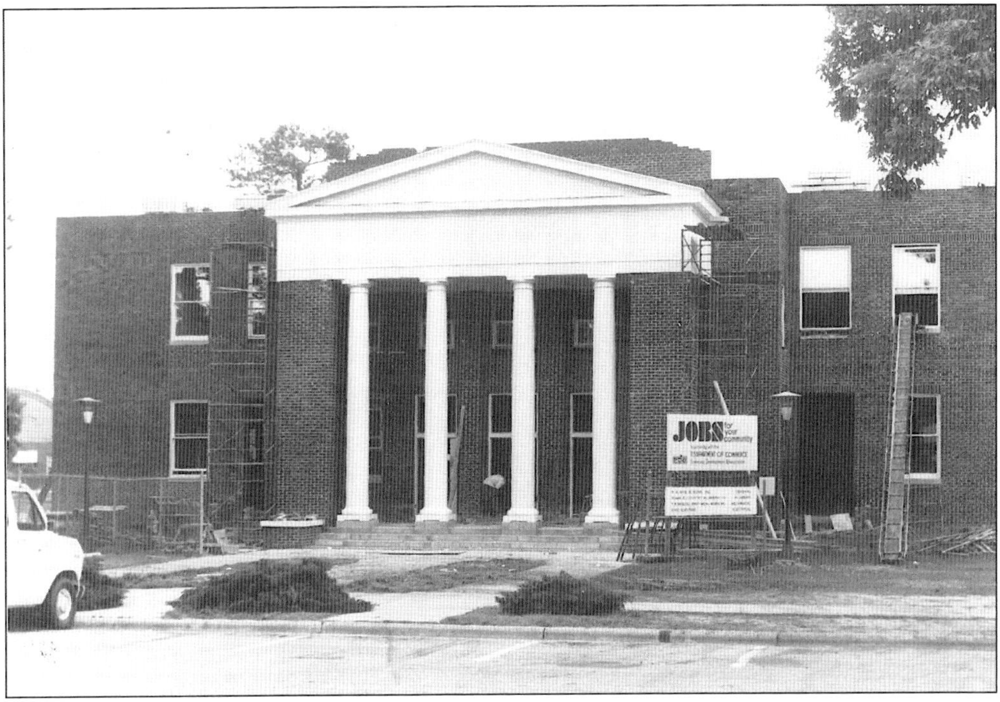

The exterior of Old Main is shown here during its reconstruction on May 23, 1979.

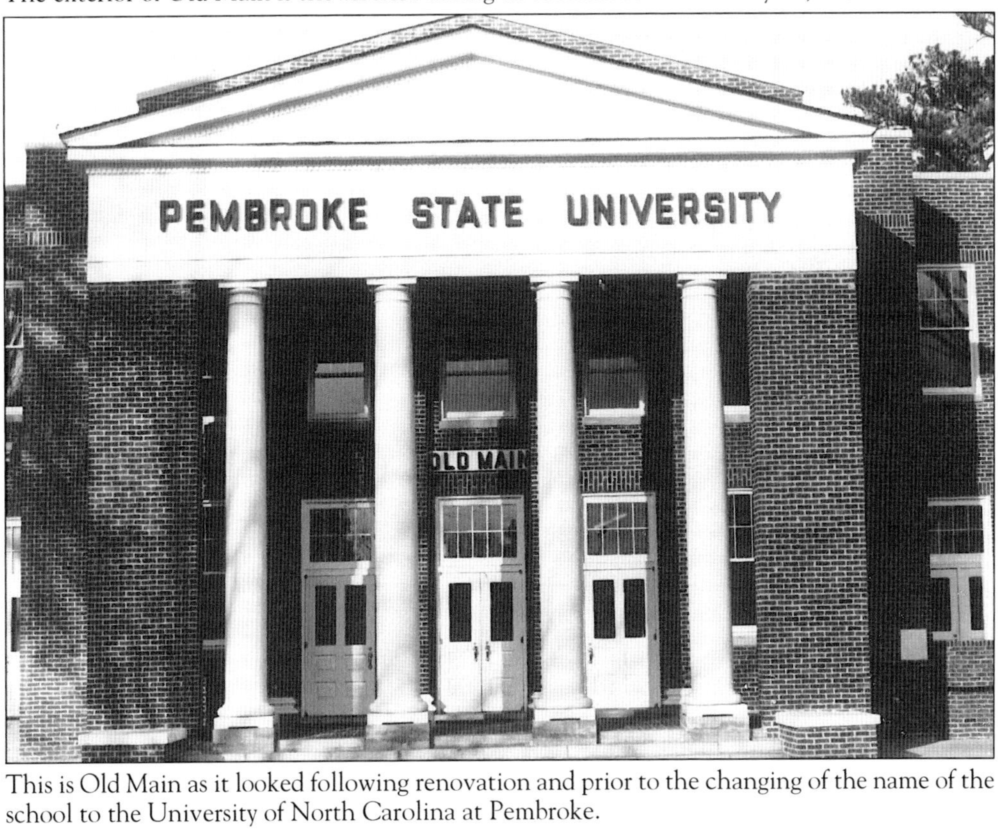

This is Old Main as it looked following renovation and prior to the changing of the name of the school to the University of North Carolina at Pembroke.

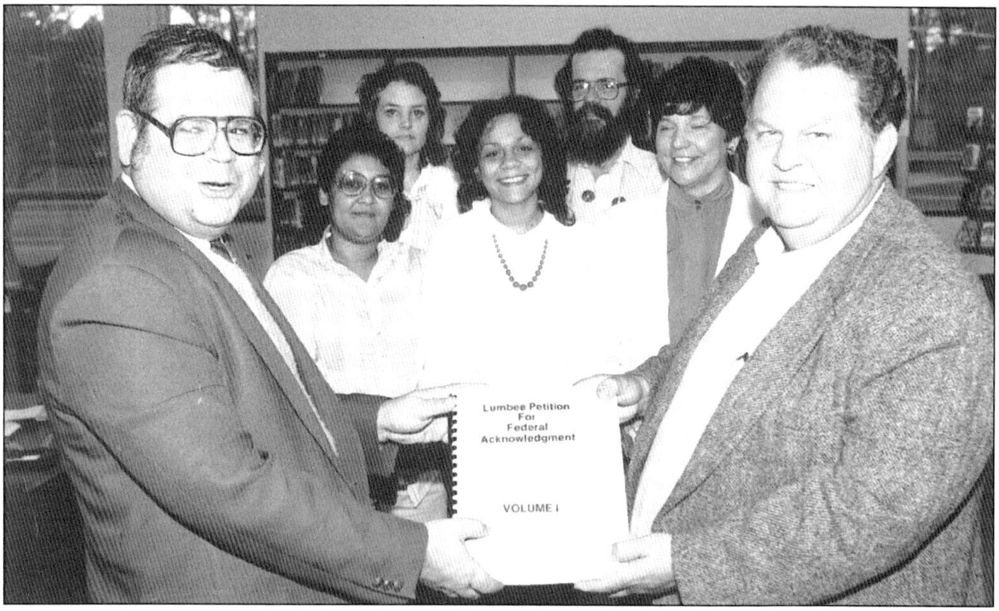

Dr. Robert Hersch (above left), the director of Pembroke State University's library services, is presented a copy of the "Lumbee Petition for Federal Acknowledgment" by Harold Deese, the chairman of the Lumbee Regional Development Association (LRDA). The 500-page document was presented in December 1987 in Washington, D.C. Shown in the background, from left to right, are Janice Locklear, tribal genealogist; Ruth B. Locklear, director of Lumbee tribal enrollment for LRDA; Cynthia Hunt, director of the Indian Law Unit for Lumbee River Legal Services; Wes White; and Rosa Winfree, a member of the PSU Board of Trustees.

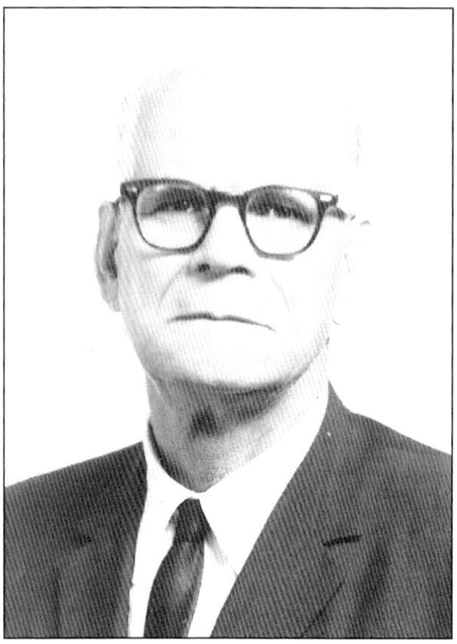

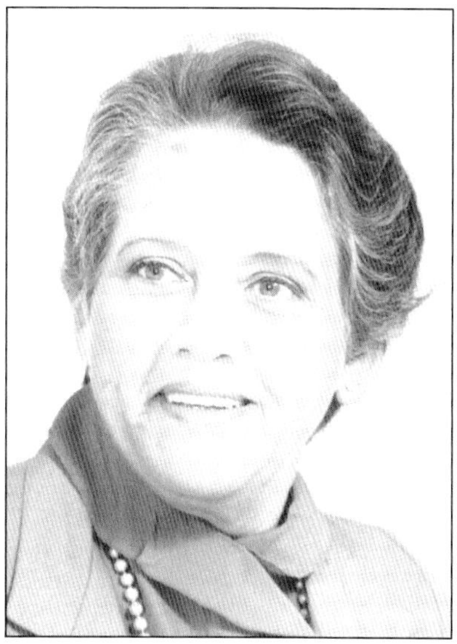

Left: This is Clifton Oxendine, professor emeritus at PSU. *Right:* Dr. Ruth Dial Woods, daughter of the late A.G. and Ruby Dial of Pembroke, is a retired educator. She was the first female Native American to be employed as associate superintendent for the Robeson County Board of Education. Following merger of the six separate school systems in the county, Dr. Woods served as assistant superintendent. She also directed the Indian Education Program. She retired recently from Fayetteville State University in nearby Fayetteville, North Carolina.

Five

Recreation

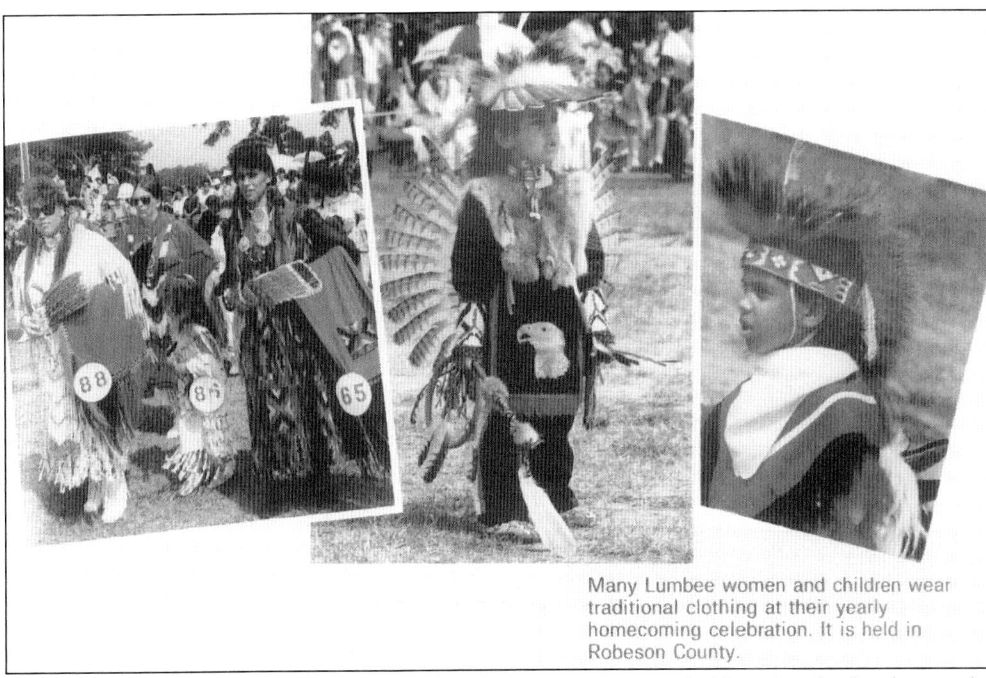

These scenes were taken at the annual Lumbee Homecoming, held in Pembroke during the Fourth of July weekend. The event is co-sponsored by the Lumbee Regional Development Association and the Town of Pembroke.

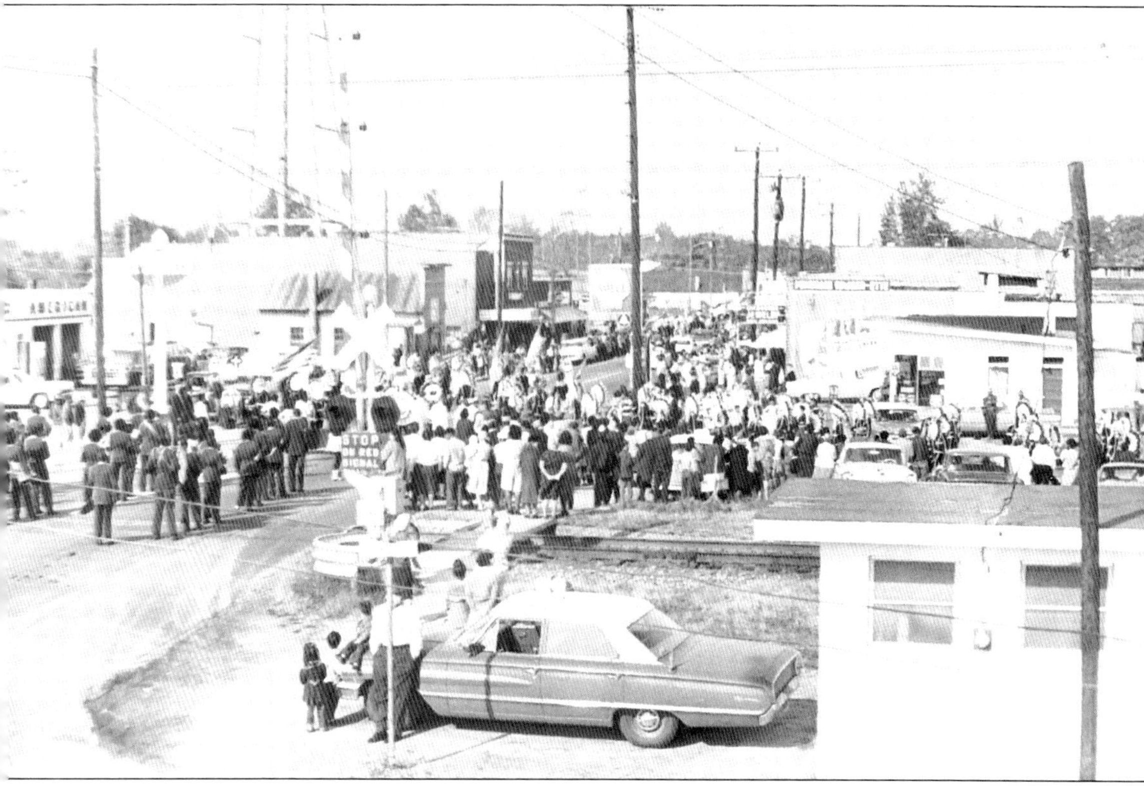

Downtown Pembroke is pictured here during a Veterans' Day parade in 1960. The Pembroke Police Department was located in the little building to the right, across from Pates Supply Company on Union Chapel Road.

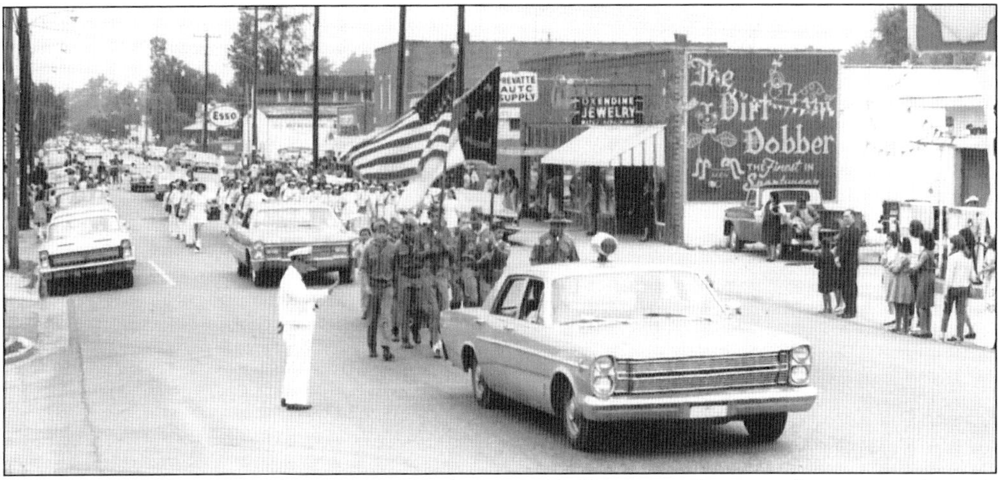

The parade is coming! This is a view of the 1960 Veterans' Day parade coming through downtown Pembroke.

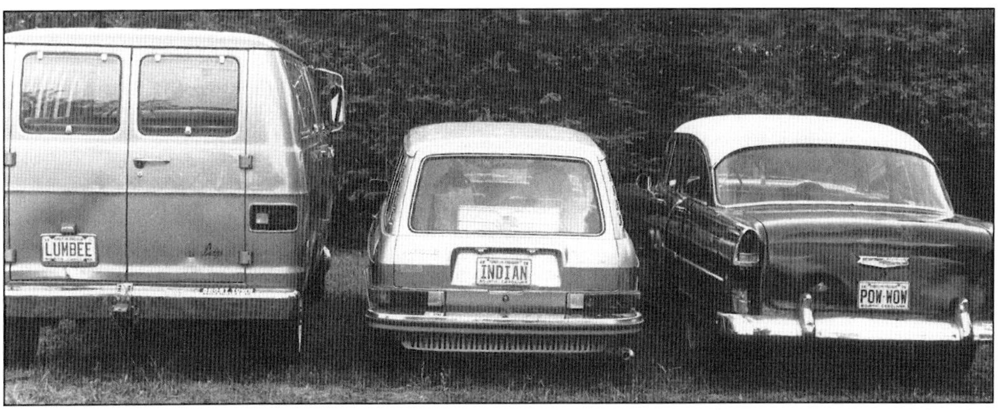

These three vehicles make a statement with their license tags. The van was owned by the late Adore Jacobs Clark. Horace Locklear and his wife, Barbara Braveboy Locklear, owned the other two. All were familiar faces and vehicles at local pow wows and especially during Lumbee Homecoming. This photo was taken in 1977. The Locklears now reside in Angier, North Carolina. Horace Locklear was the first Lumbee to pass the North Carolina State Bar Exam.

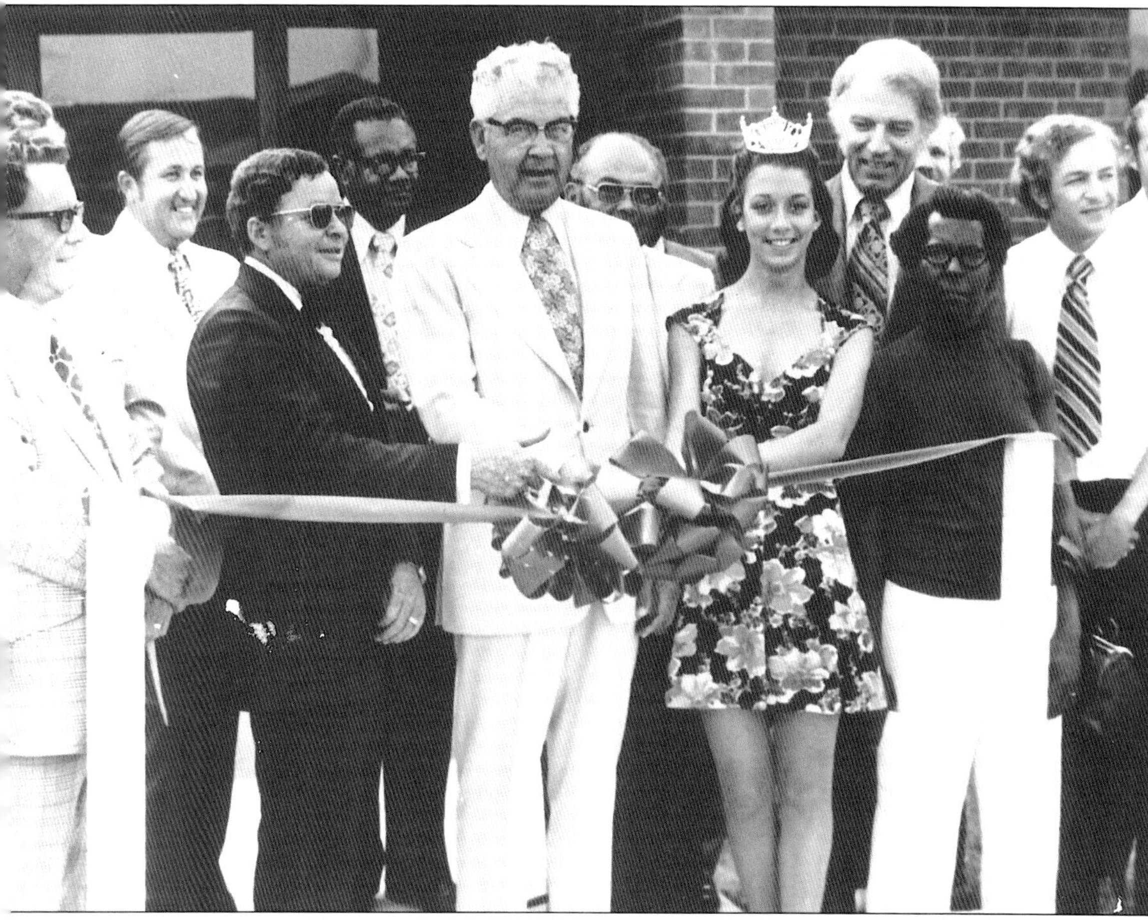

Participating in a ribbon cutting was the then "Miss Lumbee," Rebecca Malcolm. The ribbon cutting was at Maynor Manor Housing Development, which was named in honor of Earlie Maynor (center). Shown at left is Mayor Juddie A. Revels Jr.

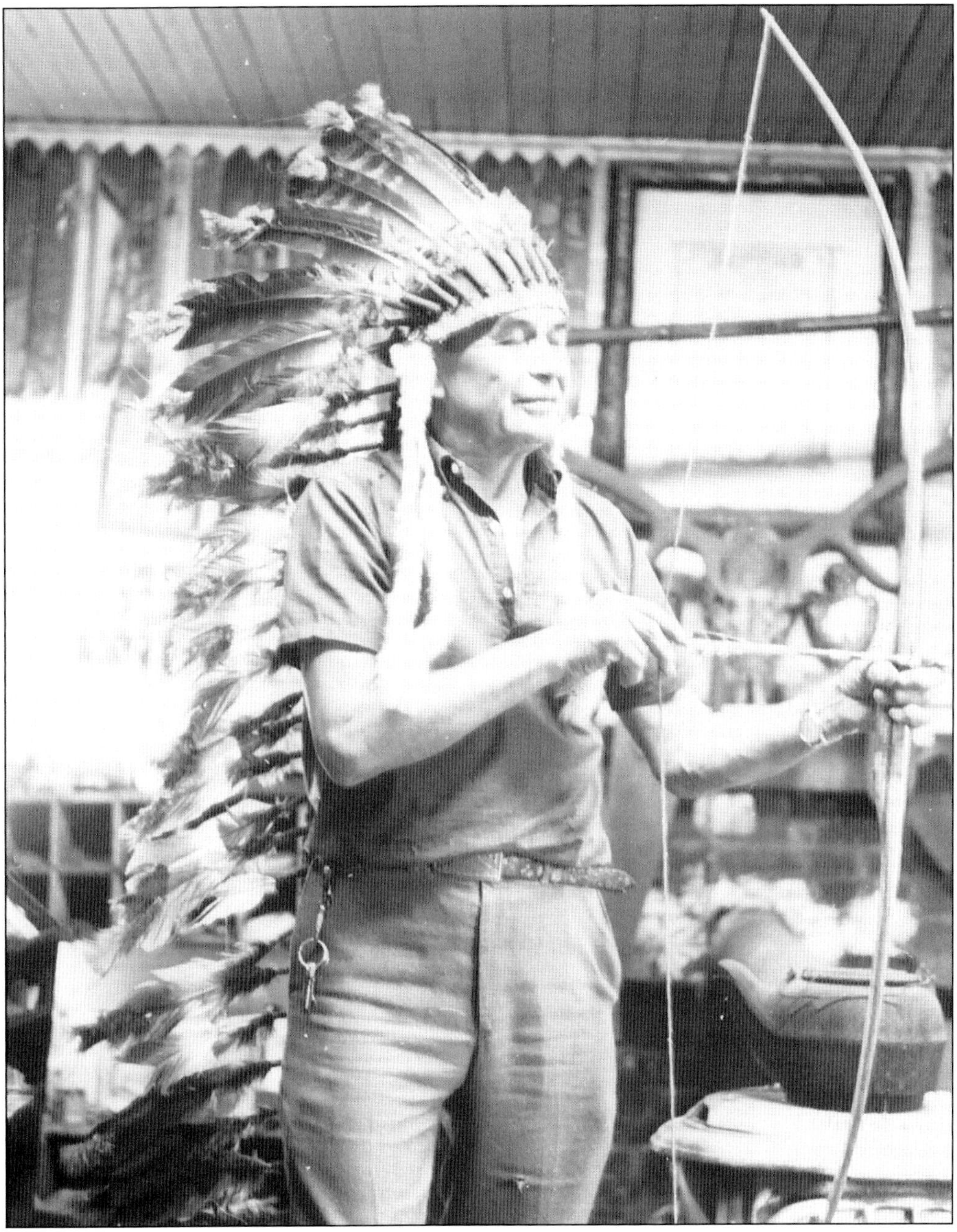

Walter Pinchbeck served as scoutmaster for Troop 327 for more than 35 years. He died in 1977. He was a Cree Indian born in 1904 in Missoula, Montana, and he came to Pembroke in 1930. Pinchbeck married Bertha Lowry, and they resided in Pembroke, near the university. Pinchbeck received the Silver Beaver Award for Scouting in 1948, and, in 1968, he was named one of the outstanding civic leaders in the United States. He received the Scouting Wood Badge in 1956 and was honored for his service to scouting by the Town of Pembroke in 1969 when "Walter Pinchbeck Day" was declared on March 31. In 1971, he was awarded a trophy as the Outstanding Indian Scout Leader in the United States. This award was presented in Bringham, Utah. Pinchbeck was affiliated with the Cape Fear Council of Boy Scouts.

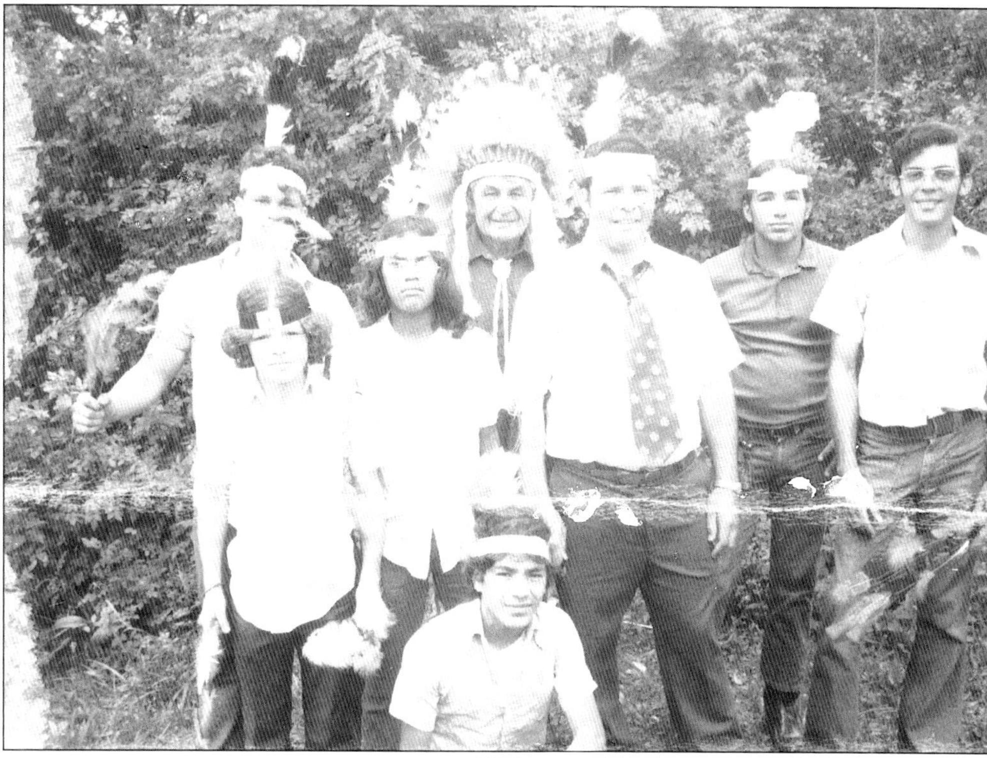

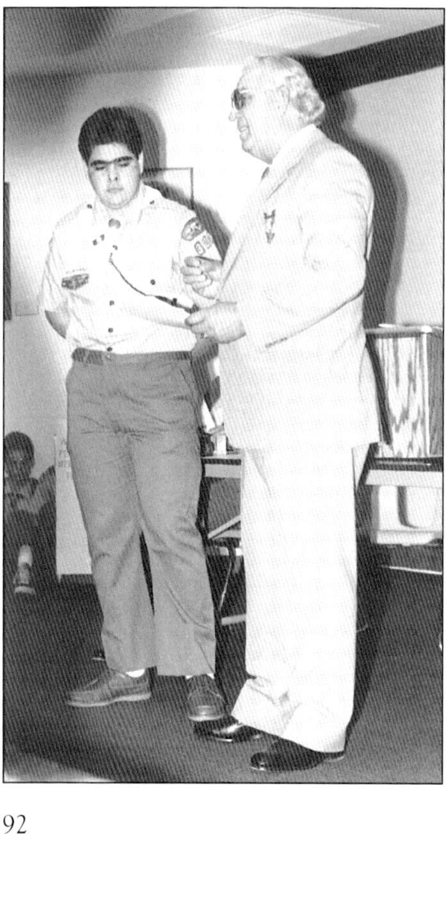

Walter Pinchbeck, scoutmaster, is shown with members of Troop 327.

Eagle Scout candidate Chuck Jacobs is shown with Scoutmaster Henry Smith. Smith served as the scoutmaster of Troop 327.

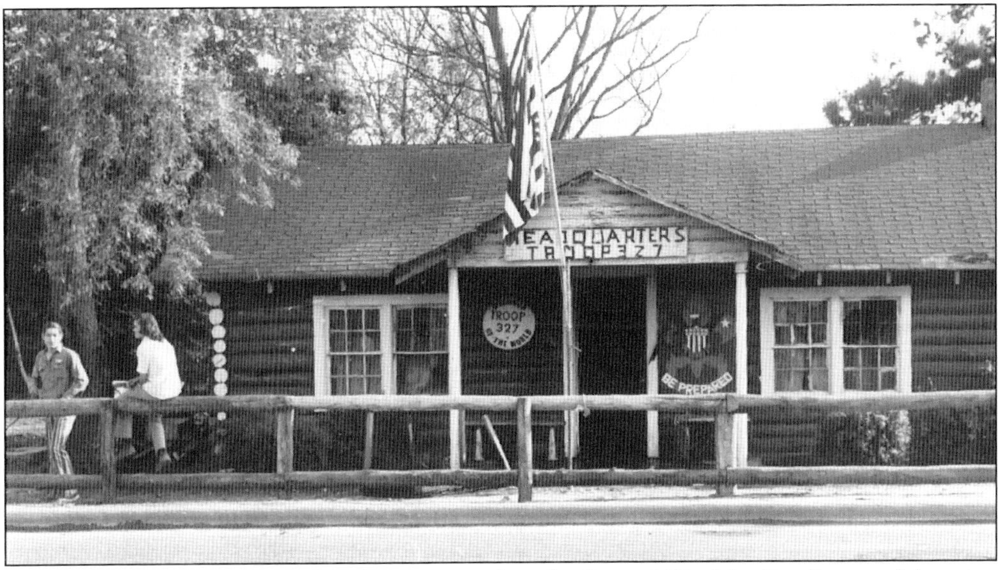

The Boy Scout Hut has served as the meeting place for Troop 327 of the Boy Scouts of America for many years. There have been 12 Eagle Scouts who have earned that distinction under the leadership of the late Walter Pinchbeck.

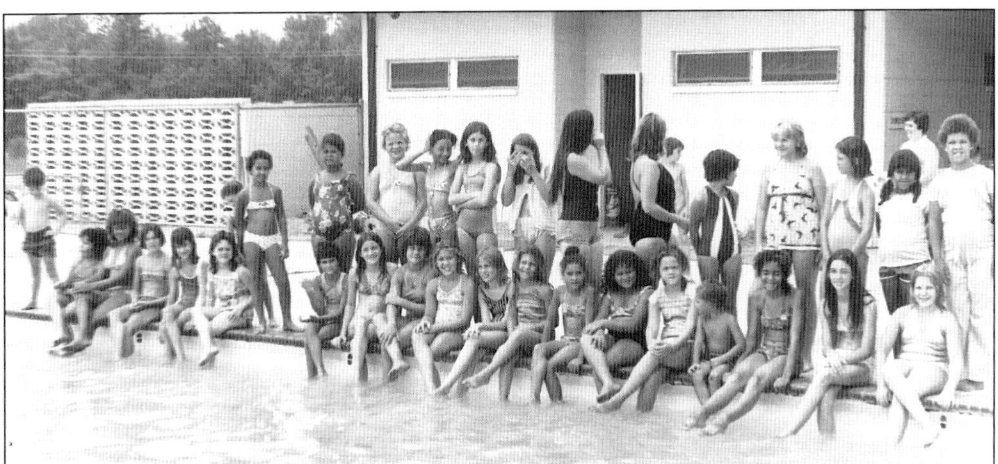

Shown here are kids enjoying the swimming pool at the Riverside Country Club in Red Banks in 1965. The Riverside Country Club is now the North Carolina Indian Cultural Center. The pool was operated by the Lumbee Regional Development Association.

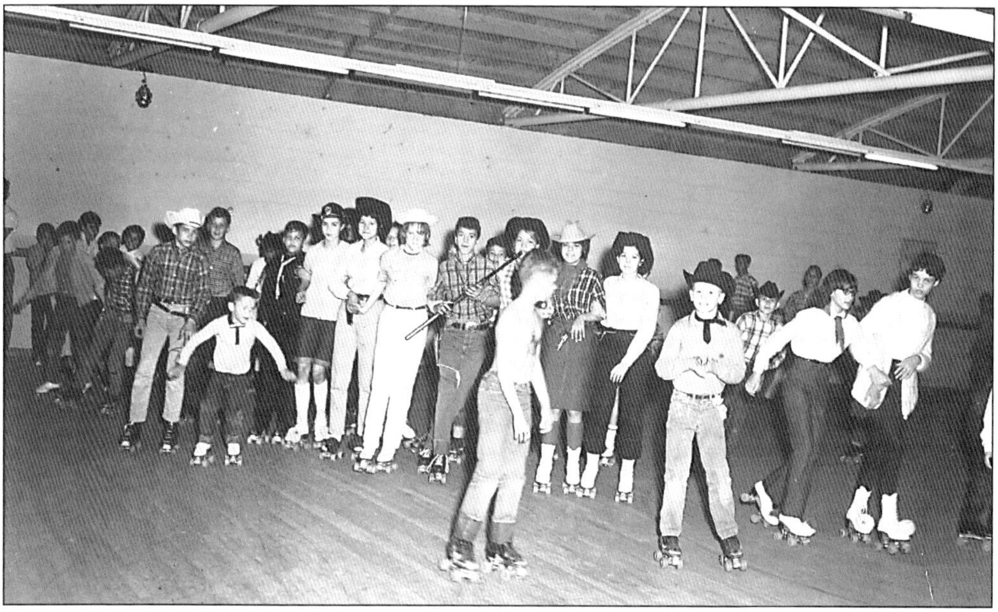

Young Lumbees are shown at the Pembroke Skating Rink, located on West Third Street, in this 1965 photo. At that time, a monthly membership at the skating rink cost only $4 per month. The skating rink was operated by James Sheffield, who, along with his wife, Janice, now owns and operates Sheff's Seafood Restaurant in Pembroke.

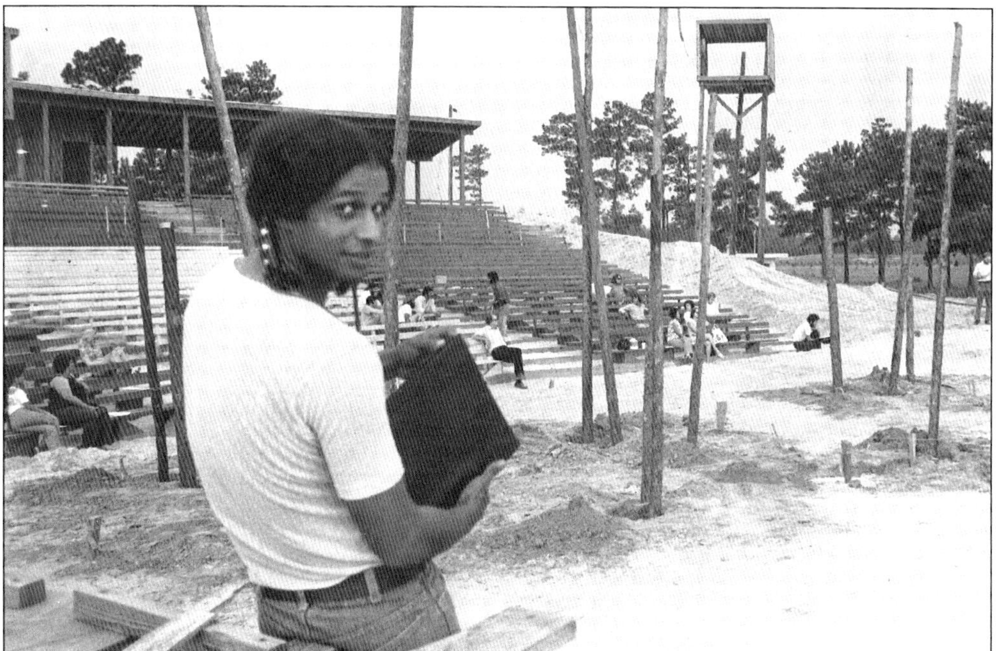

Derek Lowry is shown at the Adolph L. Dial Amphitheater at the North Carolina Indian Cultural Center. Lowry played the role of Henry Berry Lowrie in the outdoor drama *Strike at the Wind* for several years. He is shown during a relaxing moment at rehearsal in 1979.

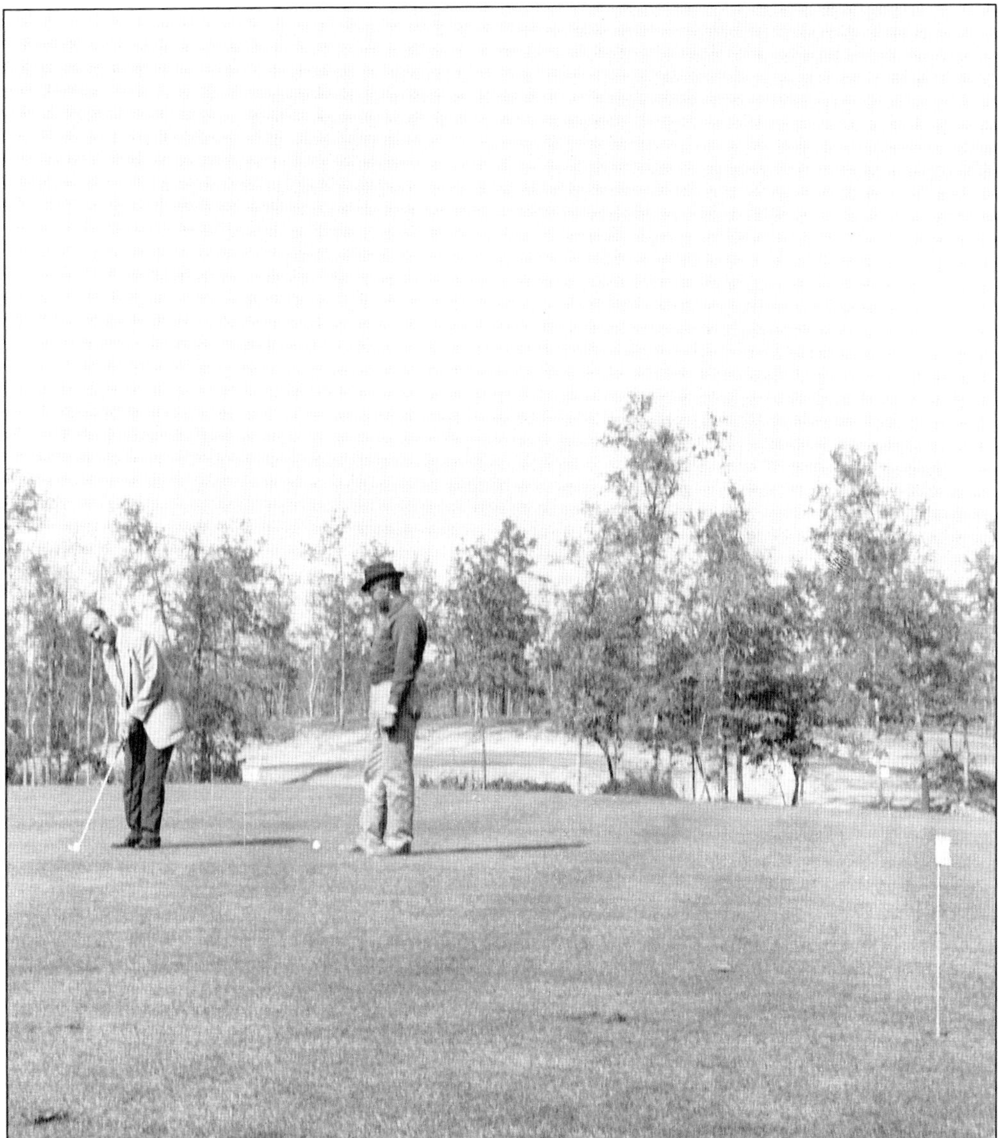

This is a scene from the Lumbee Recreation Center. The golf course began as a part of the Lumbee Recreation Center in the early 1960s. Later, the recreation complex became Riverside Country Club. It is now the North Carolina Indian Cultural Center, but the golf course remains independent and continues to operate as Riverside Golf Course.

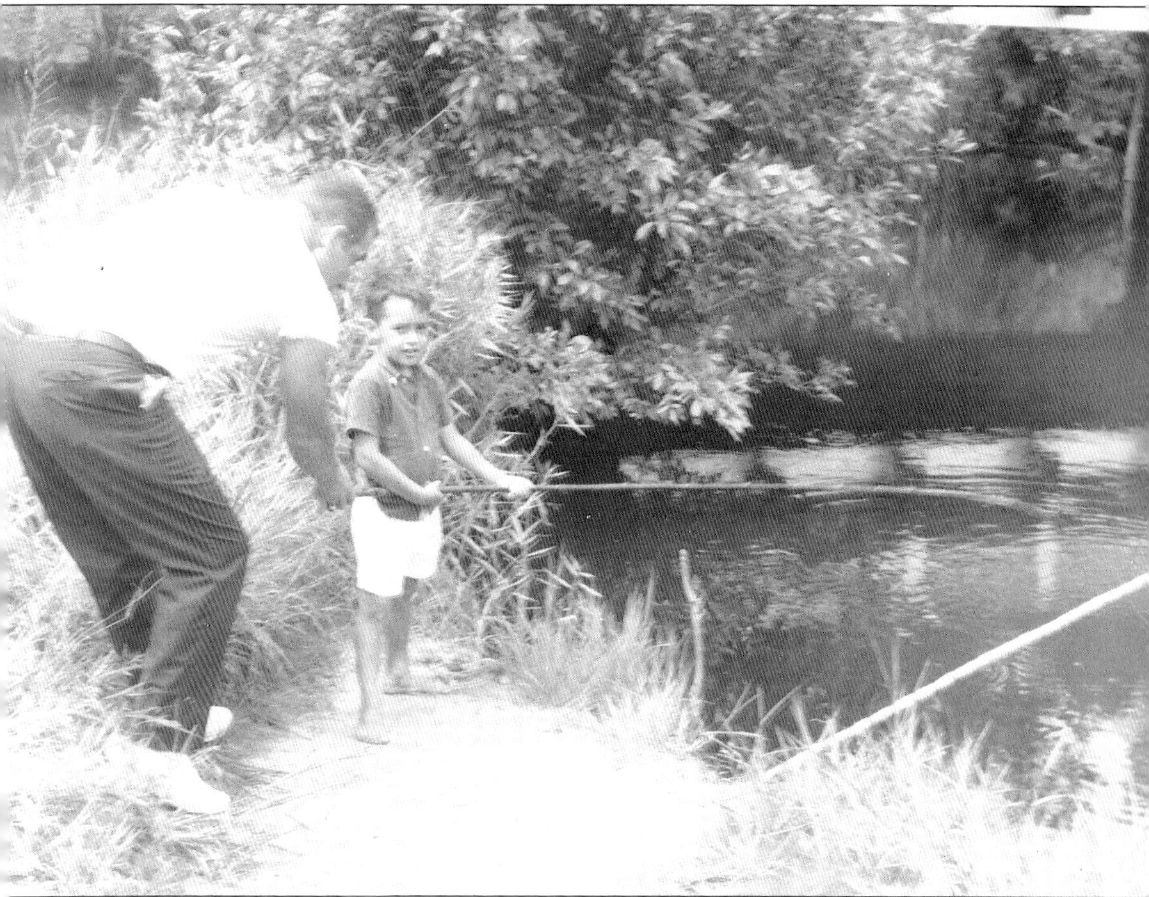

This local fishing hole is located close to the city limits of Pembroke.